THE ULTIMATE BOOK OF HOCKEY LISTS

Transcontinental Books
1100 René-Lévesque Boulevard West
24th floor
Montreal (Quebec) H3B 4X9
Tel. : 514 340-3587
Toll-free 1-866-800-2500
www.livres.transcontinental.ca

Bibliothèque et Archives nationales du Québec and Library and Archives Canada cataloguing in publication

Main entry under title :
The Ultimate Book of Hockey Lists
"The Hockey News".

ISBN 978-0-9809924-1-0

1. Hockey - Anecdotes. 2. Hockey players - Anecdotes. 3. National Hockey League - Anecdotes. I. Hockey news (Montréal, Québec).

GV847.U47 2008   796.962   C2008-941764-X

Project editor: Sam McCaig
Copy Editing: Ryan Kennedy
Proofreading: THN staff
Photo research: Glenn Levy/Getty Images
Page design: Shared Production Centre of Montreal, Transcontinental Media
Cover design: Matt Filion
Photo credits: Getty Images

Printed in Canada
© Transcontinental Books, 2008
Legal deposit — 4th quarter 2008
National Library of Quebec
National Library of Canada

We acknowledge the financial support of the Government of Canada through the Book Publishing Industry Development Program (BPIDP) and the Government of Quebec through the SODEC Tax Credit for our publishing activities.

For information on special rates for corporate libraries and wholesale purchases, please call 1-866-800-2500.

The Hockey News

Edited by Sam McCaig

THE ULTIMATE BOOK OF HOCKEY LISTS

Transcontinental Books

For Charlie Halpin, the quintessential behind-the-scenes
editor who faithfully drove the The Hockey News engine for
so many years; and, for David Fay, THN's longtime Washington Capitals
correspondent and a Hall of Fame honoree.

Acknowledgements

The Ultimate Book of Hockey Lists was the ultimate team effort, a project whose successful completion was dependent on far more than a top 10 list of contributors.

THN senior editor Sam McCaig was the point man, masterfully running the power play and ensuring the manuscript was executed on time and with flair.

THN writer/copy editor Ryan Kennedy tirelessly proofed the manuscript and fixed the mistakes.

Editor-in-chief Jason Kay held the coaching reins, deploying the troops and helping to oversee.

Graphic designer Matt Filion created the cool cover and helped secure the photos.

Upper management types – THN publisher Caroline Andrews, Transcontinental book publisher Jean Pare and consultant Arnold Gosewich – provided the necessary tools, experience, moral support and guidance for the project.

The remainder of the editorial staff bought into the concept and delivered in spades. They are: Brian Costello, Jamie Hodgson, Edward Fraser, Ryan Dixon, Rory Boylen, Mike Brophy, Ken Campbell and Adam Proteau.

Interns John Grigg, Jordan Samery, Kevin Kennedy, Sabina Lam, Justin Dickie and Patrick Soltysiak provided instrumental assistance, aiding in the writing and research.

Hockey historians/writers Pastor Glen Goodhand, Denis Gibbons, Ernie Fitzsimmons and Stan Fischler were invaluable for their knowledge of bygone eras.

Getty Images researcher Glenn Levy merits a big shout-out for helping to source the images.

And thank you to our communications/marketing team of Janis Davidson-Pressick and Carlie McGhee for helping spread the love of *The Ultimate Book of Hockey Lists*.

Table
of Contents

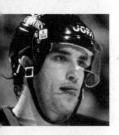
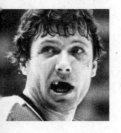

Table of Contents

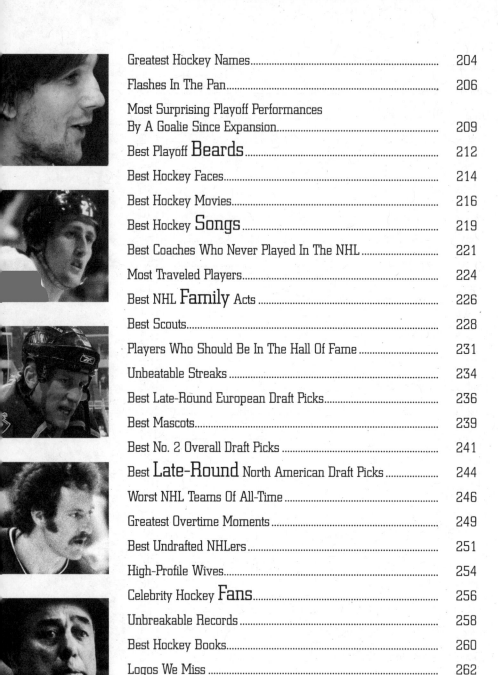

Introduction

The inspiration for *The Ultimate Book of Hockey Lists* was born five years ago, when The Hockey News published a magazine entitled *The Best of Everything in Hockey*.

It was a big-picture scan of our universe in which we focused on the pre-eminent people, places and things in our favorite game and complemented the stories with various lists. Little did we know how popular the sidebars would become.

Through word-of-mouth and reader participation we learned our core audience eats up, digests and often spits out top-10 lists; the countdowns stir debate and the passion that resides in most every hockey fan.

So, in this book, the sidebars become the main attraction, with varying degrees of meaty text to accompany the sizzle.

The ideas for the lists were developed by members of our editorial team, who then researched, ranked and wrote the segments. Unlike the NHL, we widened our net to include a range of topics, from the more serious such as top 10 players and goalies of all-time to the more frivolous, such as worst helmets ever and defunct logos we miss.

The task, while a weighty one, was a labor of love and a good learning experience. In doing the digging, we discovered/remembered things such as:

• Foster Hewitt said he almost suffocated during his first radio broadcast, having been placed in a tiny enclosure with no breathing holes. He vowed that broadcast would be his last. Fan reaction the next day changed his mind.

• Sprague Cleghorn, the game's original tough guy, was charged with aggravated assault and found guilty for clubbing an opponent over the head in 1923. He was fined $50.

• The 1970-71 Bruins dominated the scoring race, finishing first, second, third, fourth, seventh, eighth and 11th.

• Borje Salming's gruesome facial injury required more than 300 stitches to repair.

• Mike Milbury's classic zinger of agent Paul Kraus: "It's too bad he lives in the city. He's depriving some small village of a pretty good idiot."

And that's just the tip of the composite stick.

We hope you enjoy devouring the information and opinions, whether in one sitting or in bite-size pieces, as much as we did assembling them. Happy reading.

Jason Kay
Editor-in-Chief
The Hockey News

And now...
the definitive rankings
of everything hockey

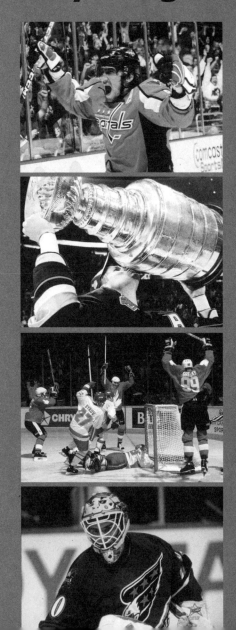

Patrick Roy

• • • Best Goalies Of All-Time

1. PATRICK ROY
Three Conn Smythe Trophies

2. TERRY SAWCHUK
103 shutouts

3. JACQUES PLANTE
Six Stanley Cups

4. DOMINIK HASEK
Six Vezina Trophies

5. MARTIN BRODEUR
538 wins...and counting

6. GLENN HALL
503 consecutive starts

7. KEN DRYDEN
Career .758 winning percentage

8. BILL DURNAN
Six-time first-team all-star

9. GEORGE HAINSWORTH
Career 1.91 goals-against average

10. BERNIE PARENT
Back-to-back Conn Smythe Trophies

The debate over the NHL's best goalie of all-time has been a two-horse race in recent years: Patrick Roy or Terry Sawchuk? An upstart, however, is starting to make his move down the home stretch. And by the time he reaches the finish line of his career, Martin Brodeur might usurp all competitors.

Terry Sawchuk

For now, though, the nod goes to St. Patrick, by a couple of crooked noses.

When Roy retired from the NHL in 2003, he ranked first all-time in regular season wins (551), enough by some standards to put him atop our list. But what really cements it for Roy is his post-season heroics. He stands alone among netminders in playoff seasons (17), wins (151) and shutouts (23) and is the only player to win the Conn Smythe Trophy as post-season MVP three times.

The first Cup run for Roy, a master of the butterfly style, was a jaw-dropper. At the age of 21, he carried the Montreal Canadiens to a storybook championship in 1986.

"When I'm in the net," he told reporters at the time. "I feel I can stop all the shots. Some nights, I make some saves that I don't even see. It's great."

MVP award No. 2 came seven years later, again with Montreal. This time, all Roy did was post 10 consecutive overtime victories en route to the Cup.

After a celebrated falling out with Montreal coach Mario Tremblay and team president Ronald Corey during an 11-1 loss on home ice to Detroit on Dec. 2, 1995 – Tremblay didn't pull Roy until after the ninth goal – Roy was traded to Colorado and proceeded to snare his third Cup. He completed his Conn Smythe hat trick five years later, backstopping the Avs to the 2001 championship.

Sawchuk was a supreme reflex goalie whose legend centers around his all-time best 103 shutouts – not to mention his sometimes surly disposition. He played 20 NHL seasons and would have posted an even more impressive win total (441) if he had the benefit of a more protracted schedule. Today's NHL schedule is 82 games; in Sawchuk's day it never surpassed 70.

Of the other greats on the list, Jacques Plante was a unique character. Every goal allowed was like a kick to the gut; he didn't make friends or socialize with his teammates; he knitted on road trips; he pioneered the art of the wandering goalie; and, of course, he broke the goalie mask barrier. Six Stanley Cup wins and an unprecedented seven Vezinas make him a no-brainer near the top of our list.

Singularity of style and character runs through the top 10 goalie greats. Dominik Hasek played a brand of goal all his own, sometimes deliberately stopping pucks with his head, other times doing the backstroke in the crease. Glenn Hall was famous for vomiting before each start. Ken Dryden was an intellectual who was in the NHL for a great time, not a long time, before resurfacing as a best-selling author and federal politician. Durnan, a late bloomer, is the only ambidextrous goalie in NHL history, while Hainsworth looked more like a door-to-door salesman than a star netminder – until the game started. He holds the league record for shutouts in a season with 22 (in a 44-game season, no less).

As for Brodeur, his quirks are less apparent, but his stats are blinding. By the time he finishes his career, he will almost certainly have surpassed Roy for all-time wins and Sawchuk for all-time shutouts.

Maurice Richard was the first, best and purest of all NHL goal-scorers. He was the first to score 50 goals in a season (in a 50-game campaign, no less) and the first to reach 500 goals for his career, and he did it while capturing the hearts and minds of all of Quebec. Images of Richard rocketing end-to-end down the rink, hair blowing in the wind, are some of the most powerful and certainly some of the most lasting in NHL history. For setting the standard by which all great goal-scorers will forever be measured, Richard comes in at No. 1.

Despite his low career goal total, Joe Malone cracks this list at No. 9 for his sheer brilliance and dominance in what was an entirely different game in an entirely different era. Malone played only 125 NHL games over seven seasons (1917-24). But as part of the rules of the early NHL, Malone scored all his goals in an era that included a rover and where forward passing was prohibited for players on offense. His 2.20 goals per game

Joe Malone

• • • • Best Pure Goal-Scorers

1. MAURICE RICHARD
544 goals, .556 goals per game

2. MIKE BOSSY
573 goals, .762 goals per game

3. BOBBY HULL
610 goals, .574 goals per game

4. BRETT HULL
741 goals, .583 goals per game

5. PHIL ESPOSITO
717 goals, .559 goals per game

6. MARIO LEMIEUX
690 goals, .754 goals per game

7. WAYNE GRETZKY
894 goals, .601 goals per game

8. PAVEL BURE
437 goals, .623 goals per game

9. JOE MALONE
146 goals, 1.17 goals per game

10. TEEMU SELANNE
552 goals, .517 goals per game

in 1917-18 (44 goals in 20 games) remains a single-season record to this day, as does his seven goals in one game in 1920. Frank Selke, the GM of the Leafs and Canadiens from the early 1930s through to the mid-'60s, once said, "Joe might have been the most prolific scorer of all-time if they would have played more games in those days."

Serge Savard starred on the blueline for the 1976-77 Montreal Canadiens.

• • • • • • Best
Teams Of All-Time

1. MONTREAL CANADIENS • 1976-77
60-8-12, most regular season points ever (132), plus-216 in goal differential, 12-2 in playoffs to win second of four consecutive Stanley Cups.

2. EDMONTON OILERS • 1983-84
57-18-5, 446 goals for, five players with 99-plus points, 15-4 in playoffs to win first of five Cups in seven seasons.

3. MONTREAL CANADIENS • 1955-56
45-15-10, three of top four regular season scorers, 8-2 in playoffs to win first of five consecutive Cups.

4. NEW YORK ISLANDERS • 1981-82
54-16-10, plus-135 in goal differential, 15-4 in playoffs (8-0 in final two rounds) to win third of four consecutive Cups.

5. DETROIT RED WINGS • 1951-52
44-14-12, Gordie Howe and Ted Lindsay finish 1-2 in regular season scoring, Terry Sawchuk plays every minute of every game, 8-0 in playoffs to win Cup.

6. BOSTON BRUINS • 1971-72
54-13-11, 330 goals for, 12-3 in playoffs to win second Cup in three seasons.

7. PHILADELPHIA FLYERS • 1974-75
51-18-1, fewest goals against, 12-5 in playoffs to win second consecutive Cup.

8. DETROIT RED WINGS • 1997-98
44-23-15, 16-6 in playoffs to win second consecutive Cup.

9. PITTSBURGH PENGUINS • 1991-92
39-32-9, Mario Lemieux and Kevin Stevens finish 1-2 in regular season scoring, 16-5 in playoffs to win second consecutive Cup.

10. TORONTO MAPLE LEAFS • 1962-63
35-23-12, second in goals for and goals against, 8-2 in playoffs to win Cup.

Sifting through 90 years of NHL hockey to come up the 10 greatest teams of all-time is no easy task. The process began with deciding which NHL dynasty – or dynasty-ish – teams were deserving of mention. The next step involved scrutinizing each to decide where they ranked. Finally, the best team from each dynasty was singled out.

The one criterion for making the list was a Stanley Cup championship. The 1970-71 Boston Bruins finished 57-14-7 with 140 more goals than any other NHL team, dominated the scoring race with six of the top 11 point-getters (including 1-2-3-4), claimed the Art Ross, Hart, Norris and Lady Byng Trophies, and had four first all-star team selections…but they don't qualify because they didn't win the Cup (Montreal did).

Another team that didn't make the list, but is deserving of special mention as one of the earliest Stanley Cup dynasty teams, is the Ottawa Silver Seven. Under a much different format than today's NHL annual playoff marathon, they won nine titles from 1903-06. During the pre-NHL days of the early 20th century, the Cup was a challenge-based trophy. Championship teams from any reputable league in Canada could duel for it and challenges had to be accepted. Multiple challenges in a single calendar year were the norm.

A portent of things to come in later decades, the Stanley Cup was largely the property of Montreal-based teams from the time it was first awarded in 1893 by Lord Stanley until the Silver Seven came along. The Seven's Cup dynasty began with a two-game, total-goals playoff victory in March, 1903, over the Montreal Victorias. Two days after vanquishing the Vics, the Seven began their first Cup defense versus the Rat Portage (later Kenora, Ont.) Thistles. Ottawa won the best-of-3 series in two games. In 1904, the Seven fended off challenges from the Winnipeg Rowing Club, the Toronto Marlboros, the Montreal Wanderers and a team from Brandon, Man.

The most famous Stanley Cup challenge ever took place in 1905. The Dawson City Nuggets traveled some 4,000 miles by dog sled, boat and train from the Yukon to Ottawa to play a best-of-5 series for the Cup. The trip took the Nuggets nearly a month. Soon after their arrival, it became apparent that, other than for the experience, they shouldn't have bothered.

The Seven handily defeated the Nuggets in Game 1 by a 9-2 score. In Game 2, things went from handily to out of hand. Ottawa superstar 'One-Eyed' Frank McGee set an unbreakable Cup record by potting 14 goals in a 23-2 rout. The contests were so one-sided the rest of the series was cancelled. The Seven's winning streak reached seven in March when Rat Portage mounted its second unsuccessful Cup challenge.

In 1906, Ottawa ran its streak to nine by winning mid-season challenges from Ontario-based Queen's University and Smiths Falls. But at the end of the 1905-06 season, the Seven finished tied for first with the Montreal Wanderers. A best-of-2, total-goals playoff was needed to award the Stanley Cup. In an exciting series featuring two mirror-opposite games, the Wanderers won 12-10 on aggregate.

And so ended one of the greatest – and oldest – dynasties in Stanley Cup history. The first incarnation of the Ottawa Senators won five Cups between 1908 and 1920, but never equaled the legendary status of the Silver Seven. And the current-day Senators? They still have a long way to go to match their predecessors.

Best NHL Coaches ● ●

1. SCOTTY BOWMAN
StL, Mtl, Buf, Pit, Det (1967-2002). Win pct.: .654; Stanley Cups: 9

2. TOE BLAKE
Mtl (1955-68). Win pct.: .634; Stanley Cups: 8

3. AL ARBOUR
StL, NYI (1970-94). Win pct.: .564; Stanley Cups: 4

4. HAP DAY
Tor (1940-50). Win pct.: .549; Stanley Cups: 5

5. GLEN SATHER
Edm, NYR (1979-2004). Win pct.: .598; Stanley Cups: 4

6. TOMMY IVAN
Det, Chi (1947-58). Win pct.: .599; Stanley Cups: 3

7. DICK IRVIN
Chi, Tor, Mtl (1928-56). Win pct.: .557; Stanley Cups: 4

8. FRED SHERO
Phi, NYR (1971-81). Win pct.: .612; Stanley Cups: 2

9. PUNCH IMLACH
Tor, Buf (1958-80). Win pct.: .533; Stanley Cups: 4

10. PAT BURNS
Mtl, Tor, Bos, NJ (1988-2005). Win pct.: .566; Stanley Cup: 1

Scotty Bowman is the Wayne Gretzky of coaches. Or Wayne Gretzky is the Scotty Bowman of players. Either way, the man with the most famous chin in hockey occupies his own realm when the discussion turns to the greatest NHL coaches of all-time.

With Bowman, it's not just the record nine Stanley Cups or all-time best .654 winning percentage. Although those numbers alone are enough to merit the No. 1 spot, it's his sustained excellence over a 30-year span that puts Bowman in his own stratosphere. Whatever the era, from the late 1960s through to the 21st century, his teams posted impressive winning records and enjoyed lengthy playoff runs. He guided his club to the Cup final 13 times, winning five championships with Montreal in the 1970s, one with Pittsburgh in 1992 and three with Detroit in 1997, '98 and 2002. Bowman's Canadiens set an NHL record with 60 wins in 1976-77, a mark that stood for almost 20 years before his Red Wings won 62 times in 1995-96.

As for longevity, he amassed 1,248 wins in 2,146 NHL games to finish well ahead of Al Arbour (782 wins in 1,607 games), the No. 2 man in both categories. Today's active leader in wins and games coached, Mike Keenan, would need to stay behind the bench for another 10 seasons and win an average of 62 games per year to catch Bowman.

Suffice to say, Bowman's records are safe.

His career began in St. Louis in 1967-68, guiding the expansion Blues to three consecutive Cup final appearances. In 1971, he moved on to Montreal, inheriting an admittedly star-studded cast, but

Scotty Bowman

Toe Blake

Al Arbour

one he was able to mold and control. After five Cups in eight years, he accepted the coach-GM job in Buffalo in 1979 and embarked on a seven-season stint that yielded the fewest successes of his career. He moved to the broadcast booth in 1987 and was inducted into the Hall of Fame as a builder in 1991 before replacing the late Bob Johnson in Pittsburgh prior to the '91-92 campaign. He acquired another Cup ring that season, followed by three more in his final NHL stop in Detroit.

Toe Blake enjoyed a scorching run of success in Montreal in the 1950s and '60s, sipping from the Cup eight times in 13 years and never failing to qualify for the post-season. While Blake had a legendary career as a head coach, he was actually inducted into the Hall of Fame as a player for his exploits with the Habs from 1934-48.

Arbour, like Bowman, got his NHL start in St. Louis before carving his legacy as the bench boss of the New York Islanders dynasty in the 1980s. He stands with Bowman and Blake as the only coaches who've guided their teams to four consecutive Stanley Cups.

Hap Day was another former star player who parlayed his expertise into a successful coaching career. He was tough on his crew (not to mention referees) and got results: five Cups in 10 years. Glen Sather was the beneficiary of the Wayne Gretzky-Mark Messier-Paul Coffey-Jari Kurri-Grant Fuhr-you-get-the-picture era in Edmonton. But like Bowman, he displayed the perfect temperament to galvanize his star galaxy.

Of course, all great coaches need great players and that was the case with the other bench bosses on this list: Dick Irvin had Rocket Richard and Co. in Montreal; Tommy Ivan was blessed with Gordie Howe; Fred Shero inherited Bobby Clarke and Bernie Parent; Punch Imlach could rely on Dave Keon and Frank Mahovlich; and, Pat Burns, the only man ever to win the Jack Adams Award as coach of the year three times (with three different teams), had the fortune of leaning on Patrick Roy and Martin Brodeur.

And what about Adams, a three-time Cup winner? He just missed the cut due to a record barely above .500 and some noteworthy crashes, specifically the 1942 collapse when his Red Wings blew a 3-0 series lead against Toronto in the Cup final.

Best Quotes ● ● ● ●

1. **"If you can't beat 'em in the alley, you won't beat 'em on the ice."**
Conn Smythe on what it takes to win in the NHL

2. **"It's too bad he lives in the city. He's depriving some small village of a pretty good idiot."**
New York Islanders GM Mike Milbury on Paul Kraus, the agent for Ziggy Palffy

3. **"We take the shortest route to the puck and arrive in ill humor."**
Philadelphia Flyers captain Bobby Clarke

4. **"I went to a fight the other night and a hockey game broke out."**
Comedian Rodney Dangerfield

5. **"I can't hear him. My two Stanley Cup rings are clogging up my ears."**
Patrick Roy's response when asked about Jeremy Roenick's trash talk

6. **"How would you like a job where, every time you make a mistake, a big red light goes on and 18,000 people boo?"**
Hall of Fame goalie Jacques Plante

7. **"Win today and we walk together forever."**
Philadelphia Flyers coach Fred Shero to his players during the 1974 Stanley Cup final

8. **"We can't win at home and we can't win on the road. My failure as coach was I couldn't think of anywhere else to play."**
Coach-turned-broadcaster Harry Neale on his days behind the bench of the Vancouver Canucks

9. **"That's so when I forget how to spell my name, I can still find my (expletive) clothes."**
Chicago Blackhawks tough guy Stu Grimson explains why he keeps a color photo of himself above his dressing room stall

10. **"Everybody talks about how unclassy I am; Fatso just forgot to shake my hand, I guess."**
Sean Avery reacts to New Jersey goalie Martin Brodeur refusing to shake his hand after the Rangers-Devils playoff series in 2008

Best GMs ● ● ● ●

1. TOMMY GORMAN
The most underrated GM in the history of the game, Gorman is the only man to win Cups with four teams as GM: Ottawa Senators (1920, '21, '23), Chicago Black Hawks (1934), Montreal Maroons (1935) and Montreal Canadiens (1944, '46).

2. SAM POLLOCK
He won 10 Stanley Cups, built the Montreal Canadiens into a powerhouse, mentored a generation of future executives and ushered the NHL through its first expansion.

3. CONN SMYTHE
The former Major ruled with an iron fist, but managed to win five Stanley Cups, built Maple Leaf Gardens during the Great Depression and is the foundation of the franchise that exists today.

4. FRANK SELKE
After building the Leafs as Smythe's right-hand man and winning two Cups in Toronto in the 1940s, Selke built the first Canadiens powerhouse with six Cups, including five in a row in the late '50s.

5. JACK ADAMS
Already in the Hall of Fame as a player, Adams was GM of the Red Wings for a remarkable 34 years and won six Stanley Cups.

6. BILL TORREY
'Bowtie Bill' built the New York Islanders from within and through the draft into a dynasty that won four straight Stanley Cups.

7. LESTER PATRICK
One of the professional game's pioneers, Patrick won Cups in the Pacific Coast League with the Vancouver Millionaires (as player-manager in 1915) and Victoria Cougars (1925) before moving to the NHL and winning three Cups with the Rangers.

8. GLEN SATHER
The former journeyman NHLer ushered the Edmonton Oilers from the WHA and built the team into one of the greatest NHL clubs of all-time. He was also a pioneer in procuring European talent.

9. KEN HOLLAND

The former minor league goaltender with a keen eye for NHL talent has won four Cups with the Red Wings and has kept Detroit a perennial contender regardless of the financial landscape.

10. PUNCH IMLACH

He led Toronto to four Cups in the 1960s, including three in a row, the most prosperous run the Leafs have ever had.

The hockey history books are not brimming with accolades for Patrick Thomas Gorman, but they should be. What Gorman did as an executive in the NHL is nothing short of remarkable.

First, he did what no other sportswriter has ever done. He put his money where his typewriter was. As an outspoken and critical sports editor for the Ottawa *Citizen* before World War I, Gorman proved he knew more than those he was covering by taking over the Ottawa Senators and assembling Stanley Cup-winning teams in 1920, '21 and '23.

After buying the Senators for $2,500, Gorman was one of the original founders of the NHL and he guided the Senators to three Stanley Cups in the first five years of the new league's existence.

After selling the Senators for cash and part-ownership in the Connaught Race Park outside Ottawa, Gorman persuaded Tex Rickard to buy the Hamilton Tigers and move them to the U.S. to become the New York Americans in 1925. He left the Americans in 1928 and made a fortune in horse racing before returning to hockey to take over the moribund Chicago Black Hawks in 1932.

He won a Cup as coach-GM of the Black Hawks in 1934, then did the same with the Montreal Maroons in 1935.

But it was with the Canadiens that Gorman did much of his best work. Those who romanticize the Canadiens and their rich history would probably be surprised to discover just how terrible the team and the franchise was throughout the Great Depression and into the early 1940s. Playing before crowds of 2,000-3,000 was not uncommon and there was often talk that the Canadiens, not the Maroons, would ultimately be the team moving out of Montreal.

Conn Symthe

In fact, when Gorman took over as GM of the Canadiens in 1940-41, the team was in shambles both on and off the ice. It was in the midst of what is known in Montreal as "The Great Darkness," a 13-year period in which the Canadiens failed to win the Stanley Cup. Lore has it that Gorman put the entire roster on waivers except Toe Blake and went about rebuilding the franchise from the bottom up.

By 1943, the Canadiens had a young Maurice Richard in the lineup and a nucleus solid enough to earn their first playoff spot in four years. The next season, the Canadiens were a powerhouse, amassing a then-record 83 points (38-5-7) and cruising to the Stanley Cup.

Under Gorman's guidance, the Canadiens won the Cup again in 1945-46 and had built up a stable of promising players that was the envy of the league. But a running feud with Canadiens president Donat Raymond came to a head and Gorman left the organization that summer.

People such as Frank Selke and Sam Pollock have since been given well-deserved icon status for their parts in the Canadiens dynasty while Gorman's accomplishments have gone relatively unacknowledged. Which is a shame, because without Gorman, none of it might have ever happened.

Best ●●●●●●
International Moments

1. CANADA CUP • 1987
Quite simply, the greatest exhibition of hockey to date.

2. MIRACLE ON ICE • 1980
Team USA's upset of mighty Soviets and gold medal victory spawns a world hockey power.

3. WORLD CHAMPIONSHIP • 1954
Soviets shock the world and Canada, and begin the most dominating era in international hockey history.

4. MONTREAL CANADIENS VS. RED ARMY • 1975
New Year's Eve classic is perhaps the most compelling game ever played.

5. SUMMIT SERIES • 1972
Calm down everyone. It was a classic series that spawned international hockey as we know it, but only one country cared about it.

6. OLYMPICS • 1998
The Czech Republic's Dominik Hasek dominates the first-ever Games involving NHL players.

7. WORLD CHAMPIONSHIP • 2002
After working its way up from the C Pool, tiny Slovakia wins its first world title.

8. WORLD CHAMPIONSHIP • 1969
Just months after Soviet tanks rolled into Prague, the Czechoslovakians inspire their nation by defeating the Soviets twice in Stockholm.

9. OLYMPICS • 2002
Fifty years to the day since its last gold medal, Canada is tops in Salt Lake City.

10. SEPTEMBER • 1972
Although a few Europeans are sprinkled around the NHL, the World Hockey Association starts play and opens the floodgates for Europeans in North American pro hockey.

Team Canada celebrates victory in the 1972 Summit Series.

Wayne Gretzky claims it was the best hockey he has ever played. It launched Mario Lemieux as a legitimate superstar and introduced the world to an unknown, young and unorthodox Czechoslovakian goaltender by the name of Dominik Hasek.

How could anything ever top the 1987 Canada Cup? It's generally acknowledged the game has never been played at a higher level than it was in the best-of-3 Canada-Russia final in that tournament, with Game 2 singled out as perhaps the best game ever played.

"I don't think you'll ever see better hockey than was played in that series," Gretzky said. "For me, it was probably the best hockey I've ever played."

Gretzky led all tournament scorers with three goals and 21 points in nine games and brought out the best in Lemieux, who had been considered a wildly talented underachiever to that point in his career. Gretzky had five assists in Game 2 – including one on Lemieux's deciding goal 10:07 into double overtime – and played perhaps his best game ever.

"His first two Canada Cups weren't Gretzky classics," said John Muckler, an assistant coach with Canada, "but he's making this one something nobody is going to forget."

The Canadian team had a total of 10 Hall of Famers and was so strong that there wasn't any room for the likes of Patrick Roy, Steve Yzerman, Cam Neely and Wendel Clark. What made Canada's team even more remarkable was that the 10 Hall of Famers – Gretzky, Lemieux, Mark Messier, Dale Hawerchuk, Mike Gartner, Michel Goulet, Raymond Bourque, Larry Murphy, Paul Coffey and Grant Fuhr – were at or approaching the height of their careers.

But none made his mark more than Lemieux, who also scored the dramatic game-winner in another 6-5 thriller in the deciding game. Lemieux had been chastised for opting out of playing for Canada in the past and for a mediocre showing at the Rendez-Vous '87 series against the Soviets earlier that year.

"I thought I had a lot to make up for in this Canada Cup," Lemieux said.

The Soviets, on the other hand, were just a few years removed from becoming NHL stars themselves. They were also just four years away from the breakup of the Soviet Union, but the Big Red Machine was already beginning to falter in global competition. Once a shoo-in at the world championship, the Soviets were coming off a second-place finish in the 1987 tournament in Vienna.

Still, the Soviets were loaded. Led by their fabled Green Unit of Sergei Makarov, Igor Larionov and Vladimir Krutov up front and Slava Fetisov and Alexei Kasatonov on defense, the Soviets were supplemented by a number of players who would later become good NHL players and two – Slava Bykov and Andrei Khomutov – who were drafted by the Quebec Nordiques, but instead decided to star in Switzerland.

Of all the things the 1987 Canada Cup represented, perhaps the most important was the respect that it garnered between the two best hockey-playing nations in the world. The Soviets were still clandestine and mysterious, but after battling them to three straight 6-5 games in the final – and a 3-3 tie in the round-robin – Canadian players and fans gradually began to stop seeing Soviets as "Commies" and began to appreciate them for the wonderful hockey players they were.

"The Soviets were great opponents, that's all," Coffey said, "because they stopped being the enemy for us a long time ago, if they ever really were that. When you go at each other with that much fire for three games, no one backs up an inch, and it's decided by one goal near the end, what else could you have for each other but respect?"

Biggest ● ● ● ●
Playoff Upsets

1. LOS ANGELES OVER EDMONTON 3-2, 1982 FIRST ROUND
48-point difference in regular season

2. MONTREAL OVER DETROIT 4-2, 1951 SEMIFINAL
36-point difference in regular season

3. MINNESOTA OVER CHICAGO 4-2, 1991 FIRST ROUND
38-point difference in regular season

4. EDMONTON OVER MONTREAL 3-0, 1981 FIRST ROUND
No. 14 seed sweeps No. 3 seed

5. SAN JOSE OVER DETROIT 4-3, 1994 FIRST ROUND
No. 8-seeded Sharks, in first playoff appearance,
beat No. 1-ranked Red Wings

6. MONTREAL OVER BOSTON 4-2, 2002 FIRST ROUND
No. 8 seed beats No. 1 seed

7. ANAHEIM OVER DETROIT 4-0, 2003 FIRST ROUND
No. 7 seed sweeps No. 2 seed

8. NY RANGERS OVER ST. LOUIS 4-2, 1981 QUARTERFINAL
33-point difference in regular season

9. NY ISLANDERS OVER PITTSBURGH 4-3, 1993 QUARTERFINAL
Unlikely Isles, with 32 fewer points in regular season,
end Pens' bid for third straight Cup

10. TORONTO OVER DETROIT 4-3, 1942 STANLEY CUP FINAL
Leafs rally from 3-0 series deficit for all-time playoff comeback

They call it the 'Miracle on Manchester,' an upset so incomprehensible it will surely never be repeated. In the spring of 1982, Los Angeles entered into its first round playoff matchup as a huge underdog against powerhouse Edmonton. The

Kings (24-41-15, 63 points) had 48 fewer points in the regular season than the Oilers (48-17-15, 111 points) and Edmonton featured the NHL scoring leader in a young Wayne Gretzky, who had eviscerated the league for 92 goals and 212 points that year. But the plucky Kings came to play and that was no more evident than in Game 3, when the purple-and-gold erased a 5-0 third period deficit and went on to win 6-5 in overtime and, two games later, captured the best-of-5 series.

Similar upsets, if slightly less dramatic, can be found throughout the game's history, which is why it really isn't over until it's over. Just ask the 1942 Red Wings or 1975 Penguins, who built 3-0 series leads over the Leafs and Islanders, respectively, before losing in seven games.

Wayne Gretzky

Best ●●●●
European NHLers

1. NICKLAS LIDSTROM
Many think he ranks as the second-best defenseman all-time behind Bobby Orr.

2. JAROMIR JAGR
Won five scoring titles, two Stanley Cups.

3. DOMINIK HASEK
Six Vezinas and two Hart Trophies.

4. PETER STASTNY
Hall of Famer ranked 56th on The Hockey News' top 100 players of all-time.

5. JARI KURRI
The first Finn ever inducted into the Hall of Fame.

6. PETER FORSBERG
Led playoffs in scoring one year despite missing the final with injuries.

7. BORJE SALMING
Brave Swede blazed a trail for others to follow.

8. PAVEL BURE
Russian Rocket won Rocket Richard Trophy twice.

9. SERGEI FEDOROV
First Euro-born and -trained player to be named MVP.

10. VIACHESLAV FETISOV
Won two Cups, two Olympic golds, seven world championships.

The Philadelphia Flyers made it their mission to run Borje Salming out of the NHL. But the harder they pushed (and punched), the firmer Salming stood his ground. Try as they might to humble and humiliate the "chicken Swede," Salming just kept on skating...all the way into the Hall of Fame.

Salming joined the Toronto Maple Leafs in 1973, along with fellow Swede Inge Hammarstrom, and by the time he concluded his NHL career in 1990 with the Detroit Red Wings, he had amassed 150 goals, 787 points and – get this! – 1,344 penalty minutes.

Chicken Swede, eh?

"He wasn't a player from Europe," former Flyer Bobby Clarke once said. "He was a player from anywhere. When he came over, we thought we could take advantage of him…scare him…but he didn't let us."

Nobody thinks twice about Europeans nowadays. Alexander Ovechkin led the NHL in scoring and was named MVP last season while Henrik Zetterberg was the most valuable player in the playoffs. But in the early '70s, Europeans were viewed as the enemy – here to take away jobs from North Americans. They had to earn respect.

"Every game players on the other team would yell at me," Salming told The Hockey News. "Most of the times in Philadelphia, when the faceoff was near the Flyers bench, everybody was hanging over their bench screaming, 'Salming, if you touch the puck we're going to (expletive) kill you!' It wasn't easy."

He's right about that. And every European that has played in the NHL after him owes Salming a debt of gratitude.

Nicklas
Lidstrom

Most ● ● ● ●
Celebrated Goals

1. PAUL HENDERSON, Summit Series winner, Sept. 28, 1972
A nation saves face.

2. BOBBY ORR, Stanley Cup overtime clincher, May 10, 1970
Airborne Orr hockey's most enduring image.

3. MARIO LEMIEUX, Canada Cup winner, Sept. 15, 1987
Gretzky + Lemieux = Legend.

4. PETER FORSBERG, Olympic shootout move, Feb. 27, 1994
They made a stamp of it. Really.

5. MIRACLE ON ICE, Mike Eruzione helps slay Soviets, Feb. 22, 1980
It went far beyond hockey.

6. MAURICE RICHARD, 50-in-50, March 18, 1945
'The Rocket' does the unthinkable.

7. BRETT HULL, 'No Goal,' June 21, 1999
It was the best of times (in Dallas), it was the worst of times (in Buffalo).

8. BOB NYSTROM, Stanley Cup winner, May 24, 1980
A dynasty is born, in overtime.

9. BILL BARILKO, OT icon, April 21, 1951
He shoots, he scores, he tragically disappears.

10. RON HEXTALL, Dramatic empty-netter, Dec. 9, 1987
Goalie makes history.

The Miracle on Ice stands alone for its drama and impact on the hockey world. It didn't, however, feature the most celebrated goal of all-time.

When Mike Eruzione scored on a wrist shot from the high slot against Vladimir Myshkin to make it 4-3 against the Goliath Soviets at the 1980 Lake Placid Olympics, there was still 10 minutes remaining in the game; the result was in doubt. The Americans could celebrate the lead, but they couldn't revel in victory until holding off a half-period barrage. And they couldn't claim gold until beating the Finns a few days later.

By contrast, when Paul Henderson beat Vladislav Tretiak for Canada in the 1972 Summit Series to help his squad roar back from a 5-3 deficit in the third period, an entire nation was able to stop holding its breath. There were 34 seconds left, but the game was over. After some severe wound-licking earlier in the eight-game "exhibition" series, Canadians were able to fist-pump and hold their heads up high as the world leaders in the game they so love. They knocked off the surprising Soviets, winning four games, losing three and tying one.

The Boston Bruins had no ties or losses against the St. Louis Blues in the 1970 Stanley Cup final. The series was never in doubt – the Bruins outscored the Blues 16-4 in the first three games – and Bobby Orr's goal against Glenn Hall in over-time of Game 4 simply put an exclamation point on the championship and helped deliver the inevitable. Yet we continue to celebrate this goal largely because of the burning image we all have in our minds of the famous photo, snapped by news-paper shooter Ray Lussier. Orr zoomed in from the point, took a feed in the slot, deposited the puck in the net, then went airborne after being tripped by St. Louis defenseman Noel Picard. At that moment, Lussier clicked and history was made.

Mario Lemieux from Wayne Gretzky in the 1987 Canada Cup was hockey heaven. Again, the Soviets were the victims (hmmm, a common theme on this list), as net-minder Sergei Mylnikov faced a 3-on-1 with less than 90 seconds to play. Gretzky chose to feed the trailing Lemieux instead of Larry Murphy, the defenseman who'd jumped into the play (a Great decision). Lemieux buried it, top shelf, creating a Hol-lywood ending to the greatest series of hockey games ever played.

Peter Forsberg's "stamp" goal against Canada at the 1994 Olympic Games in Lillehammer accomplished a rare hat trick: it won a major championship; it did so at a critical moment (the shootout); and, it was a ground-breaking masterpiece. On the play, Forsberg streaked towards Canadian goalie Corey Hirsch, faked a deke to the far left side of the net, before quickly flipping to his backhand and depositing the puck into the empty cage. Hirsch had no chance. It's the only time the gold medal has ever been decided in a shootout.

In 1944-45, Rocket Richard accomplished a feat unimaginable at that point in the game's history: 50 goals in a 50-game season. It was a record hockey observers at the time believed would never be broken. And it stood alone for 35 years until Mike Bossy matched the feat. The Rocket's record-setting goal came against Boston's Harvey Bennett in the final game of the campaign.

Three of the other celebrated goals on our list – Bill Barilko (1951, Maple Leafs over Canadiens), Bob Nystrom (1980, Islanders over Flyers) and Brett Hull (1999, Stars over Sabres) – won Stanley Cups in overtime. For Barilko, it was the last goal he ever scored; he died that summer in a plane crash during a fishing trip. The Hull goal lives in infamy due to the sniper's skate being planted in Dominik Hasek's crease when the puck crossed the goal line.

And, in the 1987-88 season, superb puckhandling netminder Ron Hextall fired the puck nearly the length of the ice, into the Bruins empty net, becoming the first goalie in league history to shoot and score a goal.

Paul Henderson

Best ●●●●●
Small NHLers Of The Modern Era

1. MARCEL DIONNE
5-foot-9, 190 pounds

2. STAN MIKITA
5-foot-9, 169 pounds

3. TED LINDSAY
5-foot-8, 163 pounds

4. THEOREN FLEURY
5-foot-6, 180 pounds

5. MARTIN ST-LOUIS
5-foot-9, 185 pounds

6. DAVE KEON
5-foot-9, 165 pounds

7. HENRI RICHARD
5-foot-7, 160 pounds

8. YVAN COURNOYER
5-foot-7, 178 pounds

9. JOE MULLEN
5-foot-9, 180 pounds

10. PAT VERBEEK
5-foot-9, 192 pounds

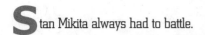

Stan Mikita always had to battle.

When he was eight years old, Stanislaus Guoth moved from the former Czechoslovakia to St. Catharines, Ont., to live with his aunt and uncle. His name became Stan Mikita, but that was probably about all he could communicate with those around him because the boy didn't speak a lick of English.

But that didn't stop him from picking up the game of hockey and making it all the way to the NHL. When he joined the Chicago Black Hawks as a teenager, a veteran on the team schooled Mikita in the ways of hockey's universal language.

"My first left winger was Ted Lindsay – a tremendous hockey player," Mikita once told the Hall of Fame. "The one thing about Teddy is he hates to lose. I looked at him one day and said, 'Teddy, you're 35 years old. You've been in this league for 16 years and you're about the same size I am. I'm a young punk kid.' I said, 'How the hell did you ever last that long?'

Martin
St-Louis

"He looked at me and said, 'Kid, hit 'em first.' I said, 'Whaddya mean, hit 'em first?' He said, 'Just don't let them run you out of the league.' "

Mikita took the message to heart. He went out of his way to prove a lack of size would-n't prevent him from playing a mean game, averaging 106 penalty minutes during his first seven NHL seasons. Mikita won the Art Ross Trophy in 1963-64 and again in '64-65; he also racked up 146 and 154 penalty minutes in those years.

Then, something changed. The next season, Mikita pared his PIMs down to 58. The year after that, he spent just 12 minutes in the box while winning the Hart, Art Ross and, yes, Lady Byng Trophies in the final season of Original Six play. He completed the impressive hat trick again the next season, making it four Art Ross Trophies in five years for the shifty center.

What makes Mikita's transformation so impressive is the fact he was able to trim so many penalties out of his game without sacrificing his trademark intensity.

"I looked at my statistics and I jotted down the two-minute penalties and what they were for," Mikita said. "The majority were what I call lazy penalties – hooking, holding, trip-ping. With an extra stride or two, I could have caught the guy and done it cleanly. Then I looked at the misconducts. One year, I must have had five or more. That's 50 min-utes right there! So, I said, 'Keep your mouth shut. Don't change your style of play, but don't take those lazy penalties and let's see what happens.' "

That philosophy served Mikita well throughout the rest of his 22-year career, spent en-tirely with the Hawks. With 1,467 points, he ranks 13th all-time among NHL scorers and behind only Marcel Dionne on this list.

With many small players, the number most frequently debated is the discrepancy between how big they say they are versus how big they really are. For instance, Mikita was listed at a very believable 169 pounds. Henri Richard must have been honest when he said he was 5-foot-7. But if Martin St-Louis is, as the *NHL Official Guide & Record Book* insists, 5-foot-9, Boston Bruins defenseman Zdeno Chara must be 10 feet tall.

All-Time Warriors ●

1. GORDIE HOWE
1,850 points and 1,685 penalty minutes in the NHL for Mr. Hockey.

2. MAURICE RICHARD
Blazing eyes exemplified his passion for the game.

3. MARK MESSIER
Only player to captain two Stanley Cup-winning teams.

4. BOBBY CLARKE
Three Hart Trophies in the 1970s.

5. EDDIE SHORE
Intense or insane? Depends who you ask.

6. TED LINDSAY
Rivalry with Maurice Richard was stuff of legend.

7. JOHN FERGUSON
Early enforcer could play, too.

8. SCOTT STEVENS
Defined entire playoff runs with his colossal hits.

9. CHRIS CHELIOS
Writing his own Greek odyssey.

10. BRYAN TROTTIER
His rodeo background showed in his approach to the game.

Being a hockey warrior isn't about just one thing. It's about synthesizing skillful and snarly attributes into a package other players naturally give extra room to because they're equally afraid of being deked out or decked.

Take the NHL's original enforcer, for example: John Ferguson joined the Montreal Canadiens in 1963-64 and immediately set about proving his hands were for more than just scoring and stickhandling. During the Canadiens' Cup-winning season in

Gordie Howe powers his way to the net.

1968-69, Ferguson skated on the left wing beside Hall of Famer Jean Beliveau. He found the back of the net 29 times and tallied 52 points in 71 games that season. He also racked up 185 penalty minutes, a single-season high for his career. Clearly, his competitive juices manifested themselves in both slugging and scoring.

That season may have been his most productive, but it wasn't far from the norm in his eight-year career with Montreal. Ferguson scored at a rate of 0.6 points per game over the course of his 500 NHL contests. "He could play the game and he brought the toughness to the team we needed," Beliveau told The Hockey News following Ferguson's passing on July 14, 2007. "There's no doubt he could contribute. Not only did he get goals, he was a very good defensive player."

Sometimes even teammates aren't safe when a warrior gets worked up.

Legendary for his talent and temper, Boston Bruins defenseman Eddie Shore nearly had his ear ripped from his head after an altercation with fellow Bruin Billy Coutu during a team practice in Shore's rookie season in 1926-27. Several doctors recommended Shore have the ear removed, but the Saskatchewan farm boy was worried about the aesthetic of being an asymmetrical blueliner. Shore refused treatment until he found a doctor willing to sew the ear back on – and even then, he rebuffed anesthesia in favor of holding a mirror so he could monitor the doctor's work and make sure it was up to snuff.

Shore, who passed away at 82 in 1985, had much more going for him than a high pain threshold. In an era when defenseman didn't do much in the way of scoring, Shore averaged just over 12 goals a season through his first five years in the league. He remains the only blueliner in NHL history to win the Hart Trophy as league MVP on four occasions.

Some of the biggest sparks in NHL history were created when warriors collided. Detroit's Ted Lindsay and Montreal's Maurice Richard despised each other during their playing days, but it was as if the two were magnetically attracted on the ice as they constantly crashed into each other.

The late Bernie 'Boom Boom' Geoffrion once recalled the intense animosity his old Montreal teammate, Richard, felt for 'Terrible Ted.'

"I remember him and Rocket, it was unbelievable," said Geoffrion during an interview for the TSN documentary series *Legends of Hockey*. "Rocket used to hate his guts, I mean, to the last degree."

As spectacular as tough guys colliding can be, things get really dangerous when they collude.

The code warriors live by was never more on display than during the Canada-Russia Summit Series in 1972. Having witnessed Valery Kharlamov chew through Team Canada like a Soviet tank through a prairie wheat field, Ferguson, an assistant coach with Canada, tapped Bobby Clarke on the bench and asked him to perform some surgery on Kharlamov's ankle. Needless to say, you don't have to ask a fella from Flin Flon twice. Clarke immediately went out and tested the durability of his stick by smashing it across the bottom of Kharlamov's leg, essentially eliminating the Russian star as a factor over the final two games of the series.

Most Hated Players ● ● ●

1. CLAUDE LEMIEUX
Mtl, NJ, Col, Phx, Dal (1984-2003)

2. SPRAGUE CLEGHORN
Ott, Tor, Mtl, Bos (1918-1928)

3. KEN LINSEMAN
Phi, Edm, Bos, Tor (1978-91)

4. KENNY REARDON
Mtl (1940-50)

5. ULF SAMUELSSON
Hfd, Pit, NYR, Det, Phi (1984-2000)

6. SEAN AVERY
Det, LA, NYR, Dal (2001-present)

7. EDDIE SHORE
Bos, NY Americans (1926-1940)

8. BILLY SMITH
LA, NYI (1971-1989)

9. DALE HUNTER
Que, Wsh, Col (1980-99)

10. BRYAN MARCHMENT
Wpg, Chi, Hfd, Edm, TB, SJ, Col, Tor, Cgy (1989-2006)

The Terrible 10 share two common traits: they were universally despised and highly successful.

Exhibit A: Claude Lemieux. He was the ultimate do-whatever-it-takes-to-win player, using his stick to score big goals and whack opponents while using his mouth to annoy foes and on at least one occasion, bite. He won four Stanley Cups with three different teams, garnering the Conn Smythe Trophy as playoff MVP with New Jersey in 1995. His legacy was cemented when, as a member of the Colorado Avalanche in the 1996 Western Conference final against Detroit, he dangerously crushed Kris Draper from behind into the boards. Draper sustained a broken jaw, nose and cheekbone and required reconstructive surgery on his face. Lemieux was suspended two playoff games and incited one of the most heated rivalries hockey has ever seen.

Sprague Cleghorn was hockey's original instigator, a rock-steady defenseman known as the master of the butt end and who wouldn't think twice about taking the law into his own hands. In one notable game against Ottawa, he forced three opponents off the ice due to injury: two via stick infractions and one with a vicious hit. The law caught up with him in 1923, when after bopping Ottawa's Lionel Hitchman in the head with his stick, Cleghorn was charged with aggravated assault, found guilty and fined $50.

Sean Avery

Ken Linseman was dubbed 'The Rat' by Flyers teammate Bob Clarke for his on-ice demeanor and appearance. He was the ultimate agitator and stickman who inherently knew how to get under the skin of his rivals, both figuratively and literally. He was also a highly effective player who had a knack for scoring big goals in the playoffs.

Kenny Reardon was consumed with winning and played the game on the Habs blueline as if his feet were on fire. He was reckless and fearless, a style that made him much-loved in Montreal and much-despised around the rest of the league. In New York, fans went as far as to form a Hate Kenny Reardon Club. Buffs of the Original Six might best remember Reardon for his long-running feud with Cal Gardner, one that featured fights with spectators and police at Madison Square Garden in one contest and subsequently climaxed when Reardon broke his rival's jaw when Gardner was a Maple Leaf.

Of the other bad boys on our list:

- Ulf Samuelsson and Bryan Marchment were notorious for borderline/dangerous hits that sometimes resulted in injury. Samulesson, also a supreme agitator, will forever be linked to a knee-on-thigh check that hastened the retirement of beloved Bruin Cam Neely. Marchment had a string of victims and earned the nickname 'Mid-Ice Madman' for his submarine-style hip checks.

- Superstar Eddie Shore, a four-time Hart Trophy winner, was a tough-as-nails defenseman whose darkest moment came when he nearly killed Toronto's Ace Bailey during a collision.

- Billy Smith wielded his substantial goal stick in the Islanders crease as if it were a machete.

- Scrappy Dale Hunter makes the list not for his plethora of penalty minutes, but primarily for his cheap shot on an unsuspecting Pierre Turgeon as the Islanders center was celebrating a game-winning playoff goal. Hunter was suspended a then-record 21 games.

- Trash-talkin' Sean Avery might eventually work his way to No. 1 on the list. He was selected as the most hated player in the league by his peers in a survey conducted by The Hockey News in 2007 – and that was a year before his stick-waving antics in front of New Jersey goalie Martin Brodeur.

Most ●●●●●
Colorful Personalities

1. EDDIE 'THE ENTERTAINER' SHACK
Clear The Track, Here Comes Shack was No. 1 song for nine weeks in 1966.

2. STEVE, JACK AND JEFF CARLSON
Slap Shot's Hanson brothers were the real deal in the minors.

3. EDDIE SHORE
Took to the ice wearing a matador's cape and played with reckless abandon.

4. GILLES GRATTON
Flakey goalie once wouldn't start a game because stars weren't aligned.

5. DAVE 'TIGER' WILLIAMS
Celebrated goals by riding broomstick-style the length of the ice.

6. GARY 'SUITCASE' SMITH
Wore a mink coat, played for 13 teams and prompted NHL to ban goalies from crossing center ice.

7. DON 'GRAPES' CHERRY
Colorful as a coach, bombastic and entertaining as an analyst.

8. FRANCIS 'KING' CLANCY
Played, coached, refereed and managed with a quick wit.

9. HOWIE YOUNG
Part-time actor once threw Frank Sinatra off a yacht.

10. FREDERIC 'CYCLONE' TAYLOR
Hockey's first superstar oozed charisma on the ice.

One of hockey's most memorable photos is a perfectly timed shot of Eddie 'The Entertainer' Shack hanging onto the shoulders of Gerry Ehman during a game in the early 1970s.

It's one of those photos you could sit and stare at for 10 minutes and peel back layer after layer of color and intrigue.

Like Shack's wide-open mouth in mid-holler. Like Shack's skates three feet off the ice whipping around the side of Ehman. One blade is slightly blurry meaning it was moving faster than the camera's shutter speed. Like the bewildered look on Ehman's face as the synapses in his frontal lobe begin to process who and what is happening to him. Like the buckling in Ehman's skate blade as it attempts to support double the 200-plus pounds it normally does. Like the staid look on the faces of the prim and proper fans way off in the distance. Did any of them crack a smile a second or two later or were they aghast that such a stunt could happen out of the blue during a game? If they knew Shack, they should have known something wacky could have happened.

It was pure cattle-rustling. On the rodeo circuit, they call it steer wrestling. Eddie Shack just calls it having fun.

In 1999, The Hockey News commissioned writers Eric Duhatschek and Bob Duff to research and report on the 100 most colorful people in hockey history. 'The Entertainer' was No. 1 on the list, ahead of such luminaries as Don Cherry, Tiger Williams and the Hanson brothers.

During a 17-year NHL career in which the Sudbury, Ont., native collected 239 goals, 465 points and 1,439 penalty minutes in 1,047 games, Shack was hockey's most colorful personality. Fans everywhere got to call him their own. He played for Toronto, the New York Rangers, Boston, Los Angeles, Buffalo and Pittsburgh. And he was a hit with fans on the road, too.

When Shack was named one of the game's three stars, he'd jump out onto the ice, make a mad dash for center ice, slam on the breaks and two puffs of snow would rise up into the air. Then he'd make a mad dash for the arena door.

"I always felt my job in hockey was to entertain," Shack told The Hockey News in 1984, nine years after retiring. "I never played seriously. I could score goals, but I knew I wasn't a natural goal-scorer. The one thing I didn't want to be remembered as was a boring hockey player."

Eddie Shack

Shack was strong, tough and didn't mind mixing it up. Part of his appeal was his working-class background. He quit school at 15, unable to read or write. He drove a coal truck and worked as a butcher before making hockey a career. And during an early contract dispute with the Rangers, Shack decided to return to Sudbury to work in a grocery store.

By the mid-1960s when Shack was hitting his prime with the Maple Leafs, Brian McFarlane and William McCauley put together a song called *Clear The Track, Here Comes Shack* and a local band called the Secrets sang it to No. 1 on Canada's top 40 for nine weeks in 1966.

"The song was bigger than the Beatles, bigger than Elvis," Shack boasted in 1999.

Shack, 71, admitted it wasn't easy always being the life of the party on the ice and at his guest-speaking functions.

"It takes a special talent to be an entertainer," he said. "I knew I had to work at it. Believe it or not, it takes a lot of time to become good at it.

"Maybe if I had worked harder and been more serious about the game itself, I might have been a more productive player. But can you imagine what you would have missed if I had gotten serious?"

Well, for one thing, we would have been deprived of the Entertainer and he would have skated around Ehman that day rather than attempt to jump over top of him.

"I got cranked up," said Shack of that memorable moment against the California Golden Seals, "and I'm going pretty good, but Ehman gets in front of me. He's bent down a bit, so I want to jump right over him. In midstream I couldn't do it, so I just had to hang on."

We're mighty glad you did, Eddie.

Best ● ● ● ● ● ●
Big-Game Goalies

1. PATRICK ROY
4 Stanley Cups, .611 playoff win pct.

2. GRANT FUHR
5 Stanley Cups, .613 playoff win pct.

3. JACQUES PLANTE
6 Stanley Cups, .634 playoff win pct.

4. BILLY SMITH
4 Stanley Cups, .667 playoff win pct.

5. MARTIN BRODEUR
3 Stanley Cups, .573 playoff win pct.

6. TERRY SAWCHUK
4 Stanley Cups, .509 playoff win pct.

7. MIKE VERNON
2 Stanley Cups, .558 playoff win pct.

8. JOHNNY BOWER
4 Stanley Cups, .608 playoff win pct.

9. KEN DRYDEN
6 Stanley Cups, .714 playoff win pct.

10. BERNIE PARENT
2 Stanley Cups, .535 playoff win pct.

Billy Smith definitely had some bear tendencies.

In addition to being more ferocious than friendly in the crease, Smith always awoke in the spring ready to do battle. And it didn't matter how deeply he'd been hibernating in the winter – once the puck dropped in the playoffs, he was ready to go.

Smith's heroics helped the New York Islanders win four straight Stanley Cups from 1980 to '83. With Smith guarding the goal, the Isles dynasty stretched through a league-record 19 straight playoff series victories, finally ending when the Edmonton Oilers beat New York in the '84 Cup final.

Talk about records that will never be broken.

In 132 career post-season games, Smith posted a .667 winning percentage. Among the goalies on this list, only Ken Dryden's mark of .714 ranks higher.

Billy Smith

New Jersey Devils coach Brent Sutter has one of the best big-game goalies at his disposal in Martin Brodeur, but also won two Stanley Cups with Smith when they were teammates on championship-winning Islanders teams in 1982 and '83.

"The best playoff goalie I've ever seen? I'll tell you what, it's tough to question Billy Smith," Sutter said. "He won four Stanley Cups on the Island. That's why everyone said he was a money goalie. Because when the money was on the line, and there wasn't much to be made back then, he took his game to a different level. He had that mindset. He was a puckstopper.

"There was something about Smitty when you got into the middle of February. He became a bear. There was a completely different focus. Everyone kind of distanced themselves from him. It was, 'Let Smitty be Smitty.' "

Smith exemplified the quality that defines all goalies on this list: No matter how they played during the regular season, they always managed to find a higher gear in the playoffs.

Overall, Mike Vernon had a sturdy but unspectacular career. However, he was a huge factor in two Stanley Cup triumphs. First, he outplayed Patrick Roy in leading his hometown Calgary Flames to the 1989 title. Eight years later, Vernon won the Conn Smythe Trophy while leading the Red Wings to their first Cup in 42 years in 1997.

As for Roy, it could be argued he's not only the pre-eminent big-game goalie of all-time, but also the best post-season performer ever, period.

No other player in NHL history can match Roy's three Conn Smythe Trophies and it's laughable to contemplate Montreal winning Cups in 1986 and '93 without him in net. He was the playoff MVP on both occasions, almost single-handedly elevating average teams to championship status. Without Roy, the Canadiens organization would be staring a 30-year Cup drought in the face.

His trade to Colorado in December of 1995 propelled a talented team over the top, as the Avs won the title in their first spring with Roy in goal. Then, in 2001, Roy bested Martin Brodeur in a seven-game showdown for the Cup, taking playoff MVP honors for a record third time. His 151 playoff wins are the most all-time (and 57 more than second-place Brodeur).

Best
Offensive
Defensemen

1. BOBBY ORR
915 points in 657 games

2. PAUL COFFEY
Recorded at least 120 points in a
season three times

3. RAY BOURQUE
Most points all-time by
a defenseman (1,579)

4. AL MACINNIS
Scored 20-plus goals
seven times

5. DOUG HARVEY
Before Orr, there was Harvey

6. PHIL HOUSLEY
Second-most points by American player (1,232)

7. DENIS POTVIN
Point-a-game D-man for 15 seasons

8. NICKLAS LIDSTROM
Mr. Everything has a slick stick and lethal shot

9. LARRY MURPHY
Great outlet passer and power play quarterback

10. LARRY ROBINSON
All-time first-team all-star on Habs blueline

Paul
Coffey

Whenever Larry Murphy got the call, it usually meant a ring.

Or two.

The slick defender was traded four times in his career, the last two paving the way for his four Stanley Cup championships.

In December of 1990, the Minnesota North Stars and Pittsburgh Penguins hooked up for a deal involving four defensemen. The Pens picked up Murphy and Peter Taglianetti in exchange for Chris Dahlquist and Jim Johnson. A few months later, Murphy was leading the Penguins to a six-game triumph over his old Minnesota teammates in the Cup final.

After winning another title in Steeltown in '92, Murphy eventually signed with the Toronto Maple Leafs. Toronto fans frustrated with the team's lackluster showing arbitrarily decided to make Murphy – the Leafs' third-leading scorer in 1995-96 – a whipping boy, booing No. 55 whenever he touched the puck. Murphy was put out of his misery with a deadline deal in 1997 that sent him to Detroit for future considerations. That promptly led to two more parades. Murphy helped push a talented Wings bunch over the top in the spring of '97, as Hockeytown won its first title since 1955. And the next year, Detroit repeated as champions.

All told, Murphy contributed 65 points in 86 post-season games during those four runs to the Cup.

As well, Murphy still holds the NHL record for points in a season by a rookie blueliner with 76 and finished his career fifth all-time in defenseman scoring with 1,216 points.

Most Bizarre Owners ●

Harold Ballard

1. HAROLD BALLARD

When he owned the Toronto Maple Leafs from 1972 to his death in 1990, Ballard ran the organization more like a circus than a hockey team with a constant barrage of sideshows that always seemed to take precedence over the on-ice product. Whether it was firing his coaches and GMs, ostracizing and trading away the team's best players, or refusing to draft players from the former Soviet Union, no NHL owner wound up in the headlines more often than 'Pal Hal.'

2. BILL WIRTZ

He always claimed to be a devout supporter of the game, but Wirtz really was always more interested in arcane business principles that handicapped his Chicago Blackhawks for decades. The liquor magnate stubbornly refused to televise Hawks home games right up until he passed away in 2007, and alienated the team's alumni and fans alike with his insistence on putting profitability before Stanley Cup championships.

3. JOHN SPANO

At the young age of 32, Spano convinced NHL brass in 1997 he was worth nearly one-quarter of a billion dollars and that he wanted to buy the New York Islanders. The league believed him at first and allowed him to run the franchise for half-a-year before the ugly truth was revealed: the man was a fraud artist who didn't have anywhere close to the amount of capital required to assume ownership. Rarely has the league been so embarrassed, which is why Gary Bettman subsequently insisted on much more stringent checking of potential owners' backgrounds.

4. CHARLES WANG

The first team owner who handed out a decade-long contract in the post-lockout NHL? Check. A man who seriously entertained the notion of putting a sumo wrestler in his team's net? Check. The person who hired a GM (Neil Smith), only to fire him mere weeks later and replace him with the team's then-backup goalie (Garth Snow)? Check. That's business as usual for the Islanders owner.

5. CHARLIE O. FINLEY

The late owner of the Oakland/California Seals franchise, Finley owned many sports teams and always left his individual imprint on them. One of his most infamous marketing decisions came when he made the team's players wear white skates, to match the appearance of major league baseball's Oakland A's, which he also owned. Finley lasted only three seasons as Seals owner before relinquishing control of the franchise to the league when he could find nobody to buy it from him.

6. NORM GREEN

Considered the savior of hockey in Minnesota when he bought the North Stars franchise in 1990, Green eventually came to be known as 'Norm Greed' when, after pressuring the city and state to build a new arena, he packed up the franchise and moved it to Dallas. The mention of his name still draws howls of hatred in Minnesota to this day.

7. THE RIGAS FAMILY

Former cable TV magnate John Rigas and his sons owned the Buffalo Sabres from 1996-2005, but wound up being stripped by the league of their ownership after they were arrested for bank, wire and securities fraud in relation to the embezzlement of more than $2 billion from their Adelphia Communications company. It seems the Spano-inspired crackdown on NHL owners wasn't working as well as the league had hoped.

8. JEREMY JACOBS

He may not be as outlandish as Ballard was, nor as creative as Wang is, but just ask Boston residents what they think of the longtime Bruins owner and then cover your ears if you don't care to hear expletives. Jacobs has penny-pinched many a Bruins legend out of a black-and-gold uniform, and as a result has never won a Stanley Cup.

9. BRUCE McNALL

Another in a long line of former NHL owners convicted of fraud, McNall was a coin collector and Hollywood movie producer who assumed majority control of the L.A. Kings in 1987 and shocked the hockey world by acquiring Wayne Gretzky from the Oilers on Aug. 9, 1988. Less than six years later, he'd defaulted on loans, was forced to sell the team and was sentenced to 70 months in prison.

10. BARRY SHENKAROW

The former owner of the Winnipeg Jets, Shenkarow maintained he did everything within his power to keep the franchise in town, but turned a tidy profit when the team was sold and moved to Phoenix.

W inning any kind of popularity contest is a gigantic longshot for the grand majority of those fortunate (and fortuned) folks who have owned an NHL team.

Unless you're someone like Red Wings owner Mike Ilitch, who delivers a Stanley Cup championship, or late Blue Jackets owner John H. McConnell, to whom local fans gave a standing ovation on a number of occasions for bringing the pro game to Columbus, odds are you'll be painted as a money-hungry businessman first and a hockey fan a distant second.

In some cases, that type of portrayal is unfair. But in other cases, it is well-deserved. And in a few select cases, the bizarre behavior of owners puts them in a league of their own. Like the 10 men listed here.

Best Old Rinks ● ● ● ●

1. THE FORUM
Montreal, 1924-96

2. CHICAGO STADIUM
Chicago, 1929-94

3. MAPLE LEAF GARDENS
Toronto, 1931-99

4. MADISON SQUARE GARDEN
New York, 1968-present (most recent incarnation of MSG)

5. BOSTON GARDEN
Boston, 1928-95

6. DETROIT OLYMPIA
Detroit, 1927-79

7. THE SPECTRUM
Philadelphia, 1967-96

8. BUFFALO MEMORIAL AUDITORIUM
Buffalo, 1970-96

9. LE COLISEE
Quebec City, 1972-95

10. WINNIPEG ARENA
Winnipeg, 1972-96

The NHL's great old barns were capable of evoking a lot of emotions, but only one could make you feel sick.

The "Philadelphia flu" would often strike teams just as their plane was touching down on the tarmac in The City of Brotherly Love. That's because there wasn't much to love about playing the rough-and-tumble Flyers in the mid-1970s, especially at the house of horrors known as the Philadelphia Spectrum. The arena was so tied to the team's reputation that its location became part of the Flyers' menacing nickname, the Broad Street Bullies.

Jim McKenny played defense for the Maple Leafs during the '70s before becoming a sportscaster in Toronto after his playing days ended. He once shared his memories of visiting the Flyers with The Hockey News.

"We'd be walking into the Philadelphia Spectrum and when we'd look over our shoulder, our bus would still be shaking," said McKenny, sort of joking.

As if facing the boys in black-and-orange wasn't bad enough, visiting clubs also had to contend with the notoriously nasty spectators who populated the Spectrum. Flyers fans love razzing opposing squads and were at their rowdy best after the late Kate Smith whipped them into a frenzy with a stirring rendition of *God Bless America* prior to the opening faceoff.

The Montreal **Forum**

One of the defining characteristics of hockey's great old venues was that each rink had its own distinct character. Unlike the many cavernous buildings that populate the NHL these days, teams used to play in arenas that dripped with charm. Imagine the Chicago Blackhawks walking up a flight of stairs for a Sunday matinee, like they used to when Bobby Hull and Stan Mikita were playing. The atmosphere at the old Boston Garden was so electric (despite the odd power failure), some fans didn't even mind the fact their view was completely obstructed by one of the building's support pillars.

Maple Leaf Gardens in Toronto was the first place that NHL fans could picture without ever actually seeing it thanks to legendary play-by-play man Foster Hewitt, whose words flowed from his perch high above the Garden ice to the far reaches of North America due to the magic of radio.

The most mystical of hockey's temples was in Montreal, where decades of unparalleled success created an aura unmatched in any other arena. The home-ice advantage enjoyed by the Canadiens was never more apparent than when the team was in the Stanley Cup final. Of the 35 times the Habs advanced to the championship series, only once – in 1989 against the Calgary Flames – did an opposing team clinch the Cup on Forum ice.

For all the parades Montreal has thrown, one of the most emotional nights in franchise history came when the Habs played their final game at the Forum on March 11, 1996. The outpouring of emotion by players and fans – including a thunderous six-minute standing ovation for Maurice Richard – showed just how deeply the hockey theatre at the corner of St. Catherine and Atwater had touched people's lives.

The **Hershey Bears** rule the AHL.

Best
Minor Pro Teams

1. HERSHEY BEARS (AHL)
Nine Calder Cups

2. CLEVELAND BARONS (AHL)
Nine Calder Cups

3. SPRINGFIELD INDIANS (AHL)
Seven Calder Cups

4. ROCHESTER AMERICANS (AHL)
Six Calder Cups

5. FORT WAYNE KOMETS (IHL)
Five championships

6. EDMONTON FLYERS (WHL)
Three Lester Patrick Cups

7. PROVIDENCE REDS (AHL)
Four Calder Cups

8. SEATTLE TOTEMS (WHL)
Three Lester Patrick Cups

9. JOHNSTOWN JETS (EHL)
Six Lockhart Cups

10. CHARLOTTE CHECKERS (EHL)
Three Lockhart Cups

While the histories of great NHL franchises are well documented, there is also a lot of interest out there for the heroes of the minor leagues. From Portland, Ore., to Muskegon, Mich., and Oklahoma to Mississippi, pro hockey has always had a fan base, even if the teams changed names, towns and arenas on a frequent basis.

With that said, however, a number of franchises have survived longer than their NHL counterparts and nurtured the big-name talent that would eventually play for the Stanley Cup. These are the teams that become legend on the bus circuit and have their own unique history.

Hershey, Pa., is one of those places with a long tradition of excellence in hockey. Home of the chocolate company of the same name, the American Hockey League's Hershey Bears have been intrinsically linked to both hockey and sweets. Not only does the team use chocolate brown as its primary sweater color, the team was originally known as the B'ars.

Along with nine Calder Cup championships and 11 other appearances in the final, the Bears boast an illustrious list of alumni, including Scotty Bowman, Wayne Cashman, current NHLers Mike Green and Marek Svatos, and of course, Don Cherry. Hall of Fame builder Frank Mathers also played a key role in Hershey's history as a player, coach and GM. Today, the franchise is affiliated with the Washington Capitals, and it continues to compete for titles and develop prospects.

Close behind Hershey is another early AHL powerhouse, the Cleveland Barons. A team that once attracted top-level talent, almost to the point of discouraging players from heading to the NHL, Cleveland served as an incubator for legends such as Johnny Bower, Emile Francis, Fred Shero and Babe Pratt. The Barons won nine Calder Cups – and made the final another five times – in their 36-year reign before moving to Jacksonville, Fla., in 1973. They would last just one full season in the Sunshine State before folding.

The 1960-62 Springfield Indians are the only team to ever win the Calder Cup three times in a row. The Indians have won seven titles in total (including one when they were known as the Kings) and made the AHL final two other seasons. The Indians were originally owned by cantankerous Eddie Shore, who also played on the team. Other notable alumni include Gump Worsley, Eddie Shack and Chuck Rayner.

Other AHL titans include the Rochester Americans (six championships) and Providence Reds (four). Both teams were synonymous with their cities for decades and the Amerks still play to this day. While the Reds became the Binghamton Dusters in 1977, the team had a 51-year run in Rhode Island.

But the AHL wasn't the only non-NHL loop with solid pro hockey. The Fort Wayne (Ind.) Komets have been one of the Midwest's finer success stories, plying their trade in several incarnations of the International Hockey League and winning five titles in 55 years (and, not to mention, being renowned for their classic 1960s spaceman logo).

Out west, the Edmonton Flyers and Seattle Totems were among the pride of the original Western Hockey League. The Flyers were stacked with talents such as Norm Ullman, Glenn Hall, Johnny Bucyk and Bronco Horvath, while the Totems won three championships between 1958 and 1968 and made the final on two other occasions.

And if you're going to have a western league, then there must be an eastern counterpart. In comes the Eastern Hockey League. That old circuit is where the Johnstown Jets of Pennsylvania made their hay. Along with winning six titles in the EHL, the Jets also featured the three Carlson brothers who would become hockey legends as the Hanson brothers in the film *Slap Shot*.

Another EHL team, the Charlotte Checkers, lives on today in the ECHL and has had an important impact in hockey's southern footprint.

Best ● ● ● ● ●
Bodycheckers

1. SCOTT STEVENS
Undisputed king of ding

2. ERIC LINDROS
A human bowling ball in his heyday

3. RED HORNER
Led NHL in PIMs for eight consecutive seasons in the '30s

4. BILL GADSBY
Broke Tim Horton's jaw, leg with one of the toughest hits ever

5. VLADIMIR KONSTANTINOV
Nobody was safe when 'Vlad the Impaler' was on the ice

6. BRIAN GLENNIE
Master of the hip check

7. CAM NEELY
Prototypical power forward could beat you with his stick or shoulder

8. WENDEL CLARK
A heat-seeking missile constantly in search of a target

9. TED LINDSAY
'Terrible Ted' was the quintessential do-anything-to-win player

10. DION PHANEUF
Open-ice madman may be heir apparent to Stevens

Scott Stevens

While this list was difficult to assemble and pare down to a top 10 – there easily could have been 40 or 50 – No. 1 was a no-brainer.

Scott Stevens built a Hall of Fame legacy on supreme defensive prowess and thundering bodychecks at pivotal moments. His most famous victim was the No. 2 man on our ranking, Eric Lindros. In Game 7 of the 2000 Eastern Conference final, Lindros carried the puck across the Devils blue-line, with his head down. Stevens spotted his prey, stepped up and caught No. 88 on the chin with, what was then (but would it be now?) a legal hit. Lindros immediately crumpled and may have been unconscious before he hit the ice.

Stevens, from Kitchener, Ont., also knocked senseless Anaheim's Paul Kariya, Carolina's Ron Francis, Detroit's Slava Kozlov and Philadelphia's Daymond Langkow, among many others, with sledgehammer checks in the playoffs.

The Bill Gadsby-Tim Horton collision in 1956 is remembered as one of the NHL's most violent of all-time. Gadsby, a defenseman with the Rangers, caught Horton with his head down and at full speed. Horton, who took the hit on the jaw, broke his leg in an awkward fall and almost had his career ended. Some witnesses that night at Maple Leaf Gardens said you could hear Horton's leg snap. Yikes.

Best Career Minor-Leaguers

● ● ●

1. FRED GLOVER
Fifteen stellar seasons in Cleveland (AHL) just prior to NHL expansion in 1967.

2. WILLIE MARSHALL
All-time AHL leader with 1,375 points over 20 seasons.

3. MARCEL PAILLE
Regarded as the best goalie outside the NHL throughout his career.

4. GIL MAYER
Won 346 games in the AHL, just two in the NHL.

5. FRANK MATHERS
Stalwart defenseman was a fixture for Pittsburgh Hornets and Hershey Bears.

6. BILL SWEENEY
Led the AHL in scoring three straight years, played just four NHL games.

7. LEN THORNSON
Ten of his 12 IHL seasons with Fort Wayne were 90-plus point campaigns.

8. JOCK CALLANDER
All-time IHL leader in points with 1,402.

9. GLENN RAMSEY
Named the IHL's top goalie six times in 16 seasons; never played in the NHL.

10. SCOTT GRUHL
Had 16 seasons of at least 20 goals; four with 50 or more.

A funny thing happened on Jock Callander's quest to become the International Hockey League's all-time point leader. There was a math error made in a statistics line from a past year and it wasn't caught until after the initial wave of hoopla celebrating Callander's accomplishment.

Jock Callander

It was Jan. 14, 2000, when Callander was believed to have eclipsed Len Thornson's 31-year-old record for all-time points (1,382 regular season and playoffs). The milestone was widely promoted by the IHL for months. There were count-down banners in Cleveland. A big celebration was planned at the next home game. The league was going to present Callander with a silver stick, and Thornson and representatives from the Hall of Fame were to be flown in.

Then The Hockey News intervened. In preparing a feature on Callander, The Hockey News found a mathematical and tabbing error in Callander's year-by-year stats. In Callander's first full IHL season with Muskegon in 1984-85, he had 39 goals and 107 points in 82 games, then eight goals and 13 assists for 21 points and 33 penalty minutes in 17 playoff games. These stats were reflected properly in the next four *NHL Official Guide & Record Books*. Then in the 1989-90 *NHL Guide*, a tabbing error wiped out the '8' in the playoff goals column, moving up the 13, 21 and 33 under the goals, assists and points columns and leaving penalty min-utes blank. The next two *NHL Guides* also carried these errors.

Then in the 1992-93 and subsequent *NHL Guides*, Callander's new playoff line for that 1984-85 season appeared as: 17 games, 13 goals, 21 assists, 34 points, 33 penalty minutes. Evidently, an editor noticed something wrong with the missing penalty minutes column and saw that 13 and 21 didn't add up to 33, so he added a 34 under the points column and moved 33 back to penalty minutes. Bottom line is, Callander was credited with 34 playoff points when he really only had 21.

It was a mistake The Hockey News felt bad about announcing – considering Callander's long-awaited journey and the league-wide celebration that ensued – but it was one we could not let slide.

The celebrations were put on hold. The Cleveland Lumberjacks did not rehang the countdown banners and the IHL did not restart an ad campaign touting Callander's chase. It took the 38-year-old Callander another five weeks to collect the 13 additional points he needed to eclipse Thornton's mark, but he did it in anti-climatic fashion.

"It was a lot more fun the first time," said Callander at the time. "It was good that it was found out. You don't want to break something when you never really did. I wish it would have been found out before, but it's not anyone's fault. It was a mistake made a long time ago."

Callander finished out that season and retired from hockey with 1,402 all-time points in the IHL, 20 more than Thornson. Callander also had 107 points in the Central League, making him one of hockey's most proficient producers not to have "really" made it to the NHL. Along the way, Callander did play 109 NHL games with Pittsburgh and Tampa Bay spread over four seasons.

Most of the players on this list are from the American Hockey League, the primary feeder league to the NHL. But there was a time when the IHL was considered as strong and competed on par with the AHL. That's why there's some IHL representation.

Moreover, many players on this list played prior to NHL expansion in 1967. With just six NHL teams before 1967, the best of the rest were confined to the minors. It stands to reason that a good player today has a better chance of becoming one of 700-plus NHLers than a good player in 1967 did to become one of just 120 NHLers. For a lot of players prior to expansion, they had no choice but to continue their fine careers in the AHL. Fred Glover and Willie Marshall are two excellent ex-amples, playing 20 seasons apiece away from the NHL spotlight.

Also finishing high on our list of the top minor-leaguers who never made it are goalies Marcel Paille and Gil Mayer. With NHL teams relying on just one goalie be-fore expansion, Paille and Mayer unfortunately were top-10 goalies in North Amer-ica for a long stretch, but never had the chance to shine because only six NHL jobs were available.

Logos ● ● ● ● ●
That Shouldn't
Be Messed With

1. MONTREAL CANADIENS	6. EDMONTON OILERS
2. DETROIT RED WINGS	7. NEW YORK RANGERS
3. TORONTO MAPLE LEAFS	8. PHILADELPHIA FLYERS
4. BOSTON BRUINS	9. ST. LOUIS BLUES
5. CHICAGO BLACKHAWKS	10. NEW YORK ISLANDERS

It's no surprise the top five teams and six of the top seven are Original Six squads. That being said, there is no bowing to tradition for tradition's sake. These logos made the list because of their simplicity, recognition and timelessness. None of these logos could be considered "cartoony" like many of the redesigned logos that have surfaced in the past 20 years. (Hello, Anaheim and Ottawa and Phoenix and…)

These designs do not feature fiery dragons or man-eating purple monsters on their crests, but instead use simple symbols to draw your attention to the team without making you gawk in disbelief.

Edmonton is our highest-rated non-Original Six logo and has remained predominantly unchanged since its creation (with the exception of that third jersey that was introduced a few years back…but let us never speak of that again). The word 'Oilers' in big bold letters is formed by a drop of oil leaking from above. Nothing fancy here, no smiling oil worker with a thumbs up to let us know how much fun he's having; rather, it's simple and straightforward. More teams, such as Washington's redesigned jersey, should go back to simple logos and stay away from complicated cartoony messes.

People Who Should Be NHL Commissioner ●

1. BILL DALY
NHL deputy commissioner is more prepared than anybody else for the job.

2. RENE FASEL
IIHF president would bring worldly perspective to the NHL.

3. BRENDAN SHANAHAN
Scoring star already has shown leadership in changing game after lockout.

4. BRIAN BURKE
Ducks GM has previous experience in league head office and nobody is more adept at sparring with media.

5. BOB NICHOLSON
Built an international hockey juggernaut as president of Canadian national program.

6. WAYNE GRETZKY
Could game's greatest player reproduce on-ice magic in league's front office?

7. KEN DRYDEN
Nobody is more eloquent about the sport than Habs star-turned-politician.

8. PAUL BEESTON
Former baseball bigwig is great at building consensus.

9. DANA WHITE
Architect behind Ultimate Fighting Championship could help hockey with his savvy marketing.

10. BRETT HULL
Stars co-GM understands ramifications of game's challenges, potential solutions as well as anyone.

Being the NHL commissioner is the toughest job in all of hockey. You get all the blame when something goes wrong and very little of the credit when things go right.

So it will take a thick-skinned, savvy individual to replace Gary Bettman when the current commissioner is ready to hand over the reins of power. But there are many good people who fit the bill.

The list has to start with Bill Daly, Bettman's second-in-command. Personable and pleasant, Daly has the requisite experience to fill the role and is a much better PR master than his boss.

Not far behind Daly is International Ice Hockey Federation president Rene Fasel. The native of Switzerland would raise the NHL's cachet among European fans and players – and his skills as a trained dentist might come in handy at arenas he visits.

Third on our list is Brendan Shanahan, the charismatic goal-scorer whose ideas on freeing up the game's best players already have been incorporated into the league. It wouldn't be too far a leap for him to continue improving the NHL's product from the commissioner's office.

Brian Burke and Bob Nicholson, Nos. 4 and 5, both are longtime hockey managers who've enjoyed a great deal of success. Wayne Gretzky (No. 6), Ken Dryden (No. 7) and Brett Hull (No. 10) all are NHL legends with solid plans to help the game endure and thrive.

Our eighth pick, Paul Beeston, won two World Series titles with the Toronto Blue Jays and later moved on to become a mover and shaker in Major League Baseball's head offices. His political skills surely could help bridge the gaps that still exist between certain hockey parties.

Finally, Dana White is a relative newcomer to the pro sports scene, but in his short time as president of mixed martial arts outfit Ultimate Fighting Championship, he has raised the bar for marketing a physical sport and could easily help improve the NHL's profile.

Best (Worst?) ● ● ●
Hockey Hair

1. JAROMIR JAGR	
2. RYAN SMYTH	
3. MIKE RICCI	
4. BARRY MELROSE	
5. THE HANSON BROTHERS	
6. DOUG GILMOUR	
7. BERNIE NICHOLLS	
8. MIKE MODANO	
9. LUC ROBITAILLE	
10. DAVE ANDREYCHUK	

Jaromir Jagr.

In hockey dressing rooms two decades ago, it was a badge of honor. But now, in retrospect, the players that sported them probably wouldn't mind if the photographic evidence disappeared. Hockey hair, specifically the mullet, owns a special place in the game. Short on top, long in the back, the mullet cascaded out of the backs of helmets for most of the 1980s and into the '90s. And while most of the players on this list have modernized their hairstyles, Colorado's Ryan Smyth – who once had a 101-year-old woman in Edmonton run her hands through his locks – has kept the tradition going to the present day.

Now, some hockey players have great hair – Mike Commodore's red afro being the gold standard – but only the mullet can classify as true "hockey hair." And for purposes of cultural sensitivity, a distinction needs to be made here between hockey hair and the traditional long hair worn by Native skaters such as Chris Simon.

Mike Ricci

With that established, we marvel at the ample poofs that flowed from Jaromir Jagr's helmet during his formative years in Pittsburgh, or the spike-gelled perfection of Tampa Bay coach Barry Melrose, who has yet to live down his '90s hairdo to this day.

Best Current TV Analysts

1. KELLY HRUDEY

Hockey Night in Canada commentator and former NHL goalie calmly and patiently speaks about the game as well as anyone and is the rightful heir to the Coach's Corner throne.

2. PIERRE McGUIRE

It matters not whether he's working on American or Canadian TV – nobody has a more passionate approach to broadcasting games than the one-time Whalers and Penguins coach.

3. CRAIG SIMPSON

A 10-year NHL veteran and ex-Oilers assistant coach, Simpson provides a level of commentary that is a perfect complement to similarly tremendous play-by-play man Jim Hughson on HNIC.

4. BOB McKENZIE

Canada's premier hockey journalist – and former editor-in-chief of The Hockey News – McKenzie is almost always TSN's voice of reason and one of the network's chief news-breakers.

5. MIKE MILBURY

The longtime Islanders GM and Bruins mainstay just recently moved into a full-time broadcast position, but he already has established himself as one of the most frank, funny men in the business.

Pierre McGuire, Bob McKenzie and Gord Miller

6. DARREN PANG

Former journeyman goaltender injects humor into hockey commentary.

7. JACQUES DEMERS

He won a Stanley Cup coaching the Canadiens, but some of Demers' best work has come as both a French- and English-language commentator.

8. BRIAN HAYWARD

Ducks broadcaster is renowned for his honesty and doesn't back down from it, even when it draws the ire of a noted hothead such as Sean Avery.

9. DARRYL REAUGH

The original 'Razor' only played 27 NHL games, but the former goaltender's work as a Dallas Stars analyst has drawn numerous accolades from hockey fans — and thesaurus junkies — alike.

10. DARREN ELIOT

Thrashers broadcaster and ex-NHL goalie puts forth solid work in both TV and print mediums.

Working as a television hockey analyst has turned into something of a 24-hours-a-day, seven-days-a-week, 51-and-a-half-weeks-a-year kind of job. There's always something to talk about in the world of the NHL — be it the entry draft, trade deadline, beginning of the season, playoffs, or a single game itself — which, curiously enough, leaves precious little time to actually sit down and analyze things.

But the pressures facing the modern media have not stopped the game's top analysts from providing top-notch insights and cutting-edge criticisms. Rather, the constant pressures associated with media competition have pushed all of the game's commentators to be better than ever.

And, despite rumors to the contrary, elite hockey analysts don't necessarily have to be old goalies to be great at their new jobs. Some are former coaches (Jacques Demers, Pierre McGuire), some are GMs (Mike Milbury), some are lifelong journalists (Bob McKenzie)...and some are actually former defensemen (Denis Potvin) and forwards (Ed Olczyk).

Although their individual styles are extremely diverse, what binds all the best analysts is their appreciation for the sport and those who play it. In their own way, they are the game's salesmen, teachers and soothsayers.

Best ● ● ● ● ●
Oft-Injured Players

1. BOBBY ORR
Bad knees limited the game's greatest defenseman
to 47 NHL games after he turned 27.

2. MARIO LEMIEUX
Never played a complete season in either junior hockey or the NHL
– and played 60 games or fewer in seven of his 18 pro seasons.

3. PETER FORSBERG
Lingering foot and ankle problems have sidelined him for
at least 20 games per season since 2003-04.

4. PAVEL BURE
Russian super-sniper played 70 or more games just five times during his
NHL career, but he scored at least 50 goals in each of those seasons.

5. CAM NEELY
Boston legend hit 35-goal plateau in first five years with Bruins, but played
only 162 games in final five seasons thanks to wonky knee.

6. ERIC LINDROS
The 1995 Hart Trophy winner was never quite his intimidating self after a series
of devastating concussions that contributed to his retirement at age 34.

7. TIM KERR
Shoulder woes derailed Flyers star at age 33.

8. WENDEL CLARK
Leafs mainstay a victim of his own bruising style.

9. ALEX MOGILNY
Missed at least 15 games 10 times in 16 seasons.

10. GARY ROBERTS
Sat out an entire season with a career-threatening neck injury and
was hurt for 20-plus games in seven other campaigns.

The physical nature of hockey has shortened the careers of some of the game's biggest stars.

Bobby Orr battled knee injuries beginning in his very first NHL season with the Boston Bruins, while Pittsburgh Penguins superstar Mario Lemieux had chronic back woes as well as a laundry list of other ailments.

Often, it's the wear and tear associated with a certain body part that can shorten a career (Pavel Bure's knees, Tim Kerr's shoulders); but, sometimes, a terrible disease such as cancer has sidelined hockey's best (Lemieux, Saku Koivu).

Even a particular style of play – for example, the power forward position – can limit the number of games those types of players appear in. See Neely, Cam and Clark, Wendel for Exhibits A and B.

No matter how a player came to miss a large chunk of time, a sense of sadness usually creeps into any discussion regarding talented-but-oft-injured NHLers. People forever wonder what the player in question might have achieved had he been blessed with durability.

Although injuries certainly help define the careers of the players who made our list, their on-ice accomplishments stand up on their own. And while not everyone on this list is assured of entry into the Hockey Hall of Fame, all will be remembered as tremendous talents that were dealt a cruel hand by fate.

Mario Lemieux

Most ●●●●●
Oft-Repeated Interview Cliches

1. "WE HAVE TO GO OUT THERE AND GIVE 110 PERCENT."

2. "WE GAVE IT OUR ALL, BUT THE BOUNCES JUST DIDN'T GO OUR WAY."

3. "WE HAVE TO TAKE IT ONE GAME AT A TIME."

4. "WE HAVE TO TAKE IT ONE SHIFT AT A TIME."

5. "WE JUST HAVE TO PLAY OUR GAME AND NOT WORRY ABOUT ANYTHING ELSE."

6. "WE DIDN'T PLAY A FULL 60 MINUTES."

7. "WHEN YOU PUT THE PUCK ON THE NET, GOOD THINGS ARE GOING TO HAPPEN."

8. "I CAN'T BELIEVE HE WAS AVAILABLE WHEN WE WERE PICKING."

9. "IT'S A DO-OR-DIE GAME FOR US."

10. "OUR GOALIE REALLY STOOD ON HIS HEAD TONIGHT."

We decided to have a closed-door meeting and make a list of the top 10 hockey cliches. Some of the guys were a little banged up, but at this time of year you've really got to put all your eggs in one basket and you have to play hurt.

Originally we had some other suggestions on this list, but in the end we decided it was time for a change; after all, you can't fire 20 writers. We all made a great commitment and it was a team effort. But when coming up with a list like this, our best writers really have to be our best writers.

Some of the guys didn't necessarily put any words to paper, but sometimes people do things that don't always show up on the edit-sheet. They were real warriors out there, and all these guys are great guys in the room, a real team of leaders.

This list was huge for us, you might even say it was do-or-die, and we were lucky enough to come out on top when it was completed. All the credit goes to our editor, who really pulled us through some of the tough times when we weren't performing up to our capabilities.

At the end of the day, though, it doesn't really matter what we did today or yesterday, we've got to keep working and come out tomorrow with the best list we can compile. Because tomorrow is a new day.

Sidney
Crosby

Most Intense ●●●
NHL Rivalries

1. NEW YORK RANGERS VS. NEW YORK ISLANDERS
Ask any Rangers fan to this day and they'll gladly tell you "Potvin Sucks!" (Even if you don't ask them, they'll quickly share their opinion on the hip-checking Isles defenseman.)

2. CALGARY FLAMES VS. EDMONTON OILERS
Battle of Alberta was forged in the early '80s and still burns today.

3. MONTREAL CANADIENS VS. QUEBEC NORDIQUES
It hasn't been the same since the Nords relocated to Colorado in 1995.

4. DETROIT RED WINGS VS. COLORADO AVALANCHE
Claude Lemieux introduced Kris Draper's face to the boards, and a Detroit-Denver hatred was born.

5. TORONTO MAPLE LEAFS VS. OTTAWA SENATORS
Toronto hasn't won a Stanley Cup in more than 40 years, so the Leafs have had to satisfy themselves by upsetting Ottawa in the playoffs.

6. MONTREAL CANADIENS VS. BOSTON BRUINS
It probably has something to do with the fact the Habs have dominated the Bruins in the playoffs for the past 100 years.

7. MONTREAL CANADIENS VS. TORONTO MAPLE LEAFS
Not much to report on recently, but Original Six's original enemies featured Canada's two biggest cities and some "us against them" French-English animosity.

8. BOSTON BRUINS VS. PHILADELPHIA FLYERS
It's 1975 and the Big, Bad Bruins are playing the Broad Street Bullies? Better bring bandaids.

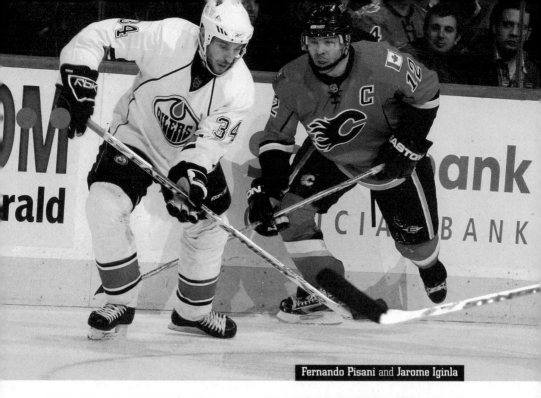

Fernando Pisani and Jarome Iginla

9. NEW YORK RANGERS VS. NEW JERSEY DEVILS

The mutual outrage can be traced back to Mark Messier's Game 6 "guarantee" in 1994; in 2008, Sean Avery took disrespect to a new level by stick-waving (and, no doubt, trash-talking) Martin Brodeur.

10. CHICAGO BLACKHAWKS VS. DETROIT RED WINGS

Even when hockey fell off the map in Chicago, they still packed 'em in whenever Detroit came to town. Old (Chuck) Norris Division rivalries never die.

From the infamous "Potvin Sucks" chant that still resonates through Madison Square Garden to the gleeful admission there are more fights in the stands than on the ice during Rangers-Islanders games, there is nothing more venomous than Manhattan versus Long Island. In the saga of New York-New York, the Isles hold a 5-3 lead in playoff series victories, but have only won one more post-season game head-to-head.

Moving north, geography also factors into the runner-up rivalry between Calgary and Edmonton. At the height of both teams' glory in the 1980s, the winner of the Battle of Alberta ultimately went on to play for the Stanley Cup (either the Flames or the Oilers made it to the final for eight straight years, from 1983-90). The sheer fact the

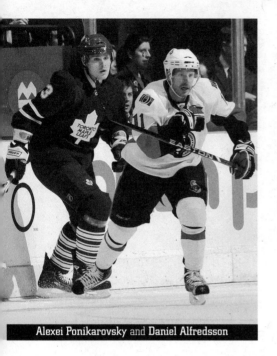

Alexei Ponikarovsky and Daniel Alfredsson

players survived those bloody Smythe Division tilts is a modern wonder. The provincial cousins still duke it out to this day, carrying on the legacies of Tim Hunter, Joel Otto, Dave Semenko and Marty McSorley. Edmonton has a 4-1 lead in playoff series showdowns.

Another heated provincial rivalry featured the Canadiens against the Nordiques. Their mutual dislike was best illustrated in a Game 6 bench-clearing brawl in the 1984 playoffs, which saw Mario Tremblay break Peter Stastny's nose and Chris Nilan and Richard Sevigny instigate third period fights after they had been officially ejected. The Habs went on to win the game and the series that night – scoring five unanswered goals in the third after Quebec's Stastny and Dale Hunter were ejected – and led the all-time playoff series 3-2 before Quebec relocated to Colorado.

With the Quebec-Montreal rivalry killed by geography, the Colorado Avalanche wasted little time starting up a new feud, this time with Detroit. Claude Lemieux's infamous hit from behind on Kris Draper during the 1996 playoffs set off a torrent of brawls and muggings between the two Western Conference powerhouses in the ensuing years. From Darren McCarty pounding on Lemieux to the Mike Vernon-Patrick Roy goalie fight, the Avs-Wings hate-fest was as toxic as they come.

The Battle of Ontario, meanwhile, has been helped along by Darcy Tucker diving into the Ottawa bench and Sens captain Daniel Alfredsson mocking Leafs captain Mats Sundin's stick-throwing incident. Chris Neil and Tie Domi could always count on extra ice time when these teams met. The talent-heavy Senators often met their playoff Waterloo at the hands of the Leafs (led by General Gary Roberts), while Toronto was consistently waxed by the Sens in the regular season, many times by lopsided scores. Mark Bell's late-season hit on Alfredsson re-ignited the flame in 2008.

The general one-sidedness of the Original Six classic between the Habs and Bruins is a pain for Boston fans and a source of joy for Montreal boosters. The two legendary squads have faced off 31 times in the playoffs – by far the most in NHL history – with the Canadiens winning 24 times, including last year's first round series which saw the Bruins claw their way to Game 7 before falling 5-0 to the once again victorious Habs. But the most famous of Boston's heartbreaks came in 1979. After losing back-to-back Stanley Cups to the Canadiens the previous two years, the B's held a 4-3 advantage in Game 7 of the semifinal, when coach Don Cherry's squad was called for too many men on the ice. Guy Lafleur would score on the ensuing power play and Yvon Lambert iced the series in overtime for an improbable Habs comeback.

Another Original Six rivalry, of course, features Montreal versus Toronto. While it's been nearly 30 years since the two clubs met in the playoffs – you've got to go back to 1979 – the Canadiens and Maple Leafs have collided in the Cup final five times, most recently in 1967 when the Leafs last claimed the Cup.

There were fireworks in the '70s when the Big, Bad Bruins went up against the Broad Street Bullies. But at no time were the stakes higher than in 1974, when Boston and Philadelphia faced off in the Stanley Cup final. The Bruins rode into the series on a 17-0-2 unbeaten streak at home against the Flyers and had home-ice advantage. But Flyers captain Bobby Clarke ended that run in Game 2 and Philadelphia went on to win its first Cup. True to the nature of the two teams, the series was littered with fighting majors and misconducts and the clubs spent the rest of the decade knocking each other out of the playoffs (and knocking each other out, period).

Martin Brodeur has befuddled many teams in his day, but he is particularly vexing for the New York Rangers. Until recently, the Devils goaltender absolutely owned the Blueshirts. In fact, from February 1997 to March 2001, New Jersey rang off a 22-game unbeaten streak (14-0-8) against New York. In retaliation, the Rangers countered with Sean Avery in the 2008 playoffs. The great agitator's instantly infamous stick- and glove-swinging routine in front of Brodeur prompted an immediate amendment to the NHL's unsportsmanlike conduct rules and added one more chapter to the heated Hudson River saga.

Toughest Fighters ● ●

1. JOHN FERGUSON
1,214 penalty minutes

2. BOB PROBERT
3,300 penalty minutes

3. DAVE 'THE HAMMER' SCHULTZ
2,294 penalty minutes

4. DAVE 'TIGER' WILLIAMS
3,966 penalty minutes

5. GEORGES LARAQUE
1,037 penalty minutes (active)

6. DAVE SEMENKO
1,175 penalty minutes

7. TIE DOMI
3,515 penalty minutes

8. TERRY O'REILLY
2,095 penalty minutes

9. MARTY McSORLEY
3,381 penalty minutes

10. STAN JONATHAN
751 penalty minutes

As the NHL's original policeman, Ferguson was as hard as they come. The man whose fists allowed the rest of his Canadiens teammates to skate without fear, Ferguson also was an effective player when his gloves were on. His best totals came in 1968-69, when he tallied 29 goals and 52 points in 71 games. The enforcer won five Stanley Cups in eight seasons and is regarded as one of the toughest NHLers ever, high praise considering he was just 6-feet and 180 pounds.

How would he have fared against Red Wings anti-hero Bob Probert (6-foot-3, 225 pounds)? We'll never know. But with today's fighters such as Georges Laraque, Derek Boogaard and Donald Brashear all coming in at well over six feet tall and 230-plus pounds, it's safe to say times have changed since Fergie's heyday.

John Ferguson

Quebec Nordiques

••• Gone-But-Not-Forgotten
NHL Teams

1. WINNIPEG JETS (1979-96)
2. QUEBEC NORDIQUES (1979-95)
3. HARTFORD WHALERS (1979-97)
4. KANSAS CITY SCOUTS (1974-76)
5. CLEVELAND BARONS (1976-78)
6. CALIFORNIA/OAKLAND SEALS (1967-76)
7. MINNESOTA NORTH STARS (1967-93)
8. ATLANTA FLAMES (1972-80)
9. COLORADO ROCKIES (1976-82)
10. OTTAWA SENATORS (1917-34)

The NHL has a history of franchise expansion and relocation, with a few false starts and collapses thrown in. Some defunct teams have lingered in the public's imagination longer than others, leading to the hope the NHL will return. And once in a while, a city gets a second chance at big-league hockey; during commissioner Gary Bettman's era, for example, several American locales have received another shot at the NHL. Canadian cities? Not so much.

If there's one city that immediately leaps to mind when it comes to a failed-but-not-forgotten market, it is Winnipeg. Home of the NHL's Jets from 1979 to 1996 (and the World Hockey Association before that), the prairie town lost out to the desert when ownership, arena issues and poor attendance saw the team flee and become the Phoenix Coyotes. While Jets fans still hold out hope of a return, any recent talks of a struggling NHL franchise moving to Winnipeg have been nixed in favor of an American town such as Kansas City. Ironically, the former home of the Scouts is one U.S. city that hasn't had an NHL sequel after a failed franchise attempt; meanwhile, Atlanta, Colorado and Minnesota have all returned to the NHL (and to a certain extent, Oakland, in the form of the San Jose Sharks).

An American city that ranks up with Winnipeg – and Quebec City, which supported a contending Nordiques team in the mid-1980s – in terms of fan nostalgia is Hartford. Another team with arena problems and a small but rabid fan base, the Whalers inspired a cult following based on their classic logo and the playing of *Brass Bonanza* at all home games.

While 'The Whale' would win a Stanley Cup as the Carolina Hurricanes a decade after relocating, it took Quebec just one season to learn true heartbreak when the Colorado Avalanche was crowned league champions in 1996, with former Habs nemesis Patrick Roy in net.

Several of the cities on the list are directly linked: when the Seals weren't working out in Oakland, they became the Cleveland Barons. When that didn't take, the Barons were absorbed into the Minnesota North Stars…who later moved to Dallas and were renamed the Stars.

In a similar but earlier movement, the original Ottawa Senators moved to St. Louis and became the Eagles in 1935, but folded one season later.

NHL Controversies ● ● ●

1. ALAN EAGLESON

Once hockey's biggest power broker, he leaves the game in disgrace in early 1990s after fraud, embezzlement convictions for misusing players' money.

2. THE RICHARD RIOTS

Montreal burns after Canadiens star Maurice Richard, who knocked out a linesman, is banned for remainder of 1954-55 regular season and playoffs.

3. 2004-05 LOCKOUT

The NHL closes down for an entire season – the first major pro sports league to do so – as owners, players wage salary war.

4. TODD BERTUZZI-STEVE MOORE

On-ice blindside attack results in premature, concussion-induced retirement for Moore and assault conviction for Bertuzzi.

5. MIKE DANTON-DAVID FROST

Bizarre relationship between player and agent comes to an end when Danton is found guilty of murder-for-hire plot targeting Frost.

6. MAPLE LEAF GARDENS SEX SCANDAL

Hockey shrine's darkest chapter as two ushers found guilty of longtime sexual abuse of teenage boys.

7. MARTY McSORLEY-DONALD BRASHEAR

The High Stick To The Head Heard 'Round The World.

8. DON CHERRY

No shortage of contentious rants over the years by Coach's Corner fixture.

9. 'NO GOAL'

Brett Hull's skate is clearly in the crease – which the league had cracked down on all season – as he scores Stanley Cup-winning goal in overtime for Dallas against Buffalo in 1999.

10. TED SASKIN

Fast-tracked hiring and email hacking spells quick exit for short-lived NHLPA boss.

For whatever reason, the NHL has been a lightning rod for controversy.

Perhaps it's the overwhelming passion for the game that burns within players and fans alike. Perhaps it's the win-at-all-costs attitude that permeates professional sports. Or perhaps there's simply bound to be problems when you've got intensely competitive athletes skating around on two knives while carrying clubs.

Whatever the case, the league has had its share of troubles, including a number of off-ice incidents that didn't even involve hockey players.

For starters, there's Don Cherry, one of the most polarizing figures in Canadian sports history (heck, Canadian history in general). He was voted No. 7 on the CBC TV special *The Greatest Canadian*, though some provinces east of Ontario and west of Newfoundland who speak a language other than English may dispute that result.

Cherry, from his podium on *Hockey Night in Canada's* Coach's Corner for the past quarter-century, has had some choice words for French-Canadians, Europeans, visors, fighting and of course, his beloved Boston Bruins and Toronto Maple Leafs. His unabashed bias for – and against – certain players and teams is something other analysts deeply frown upon, but Cherry can never be accused of being anything less than up front and uncensored.

One of his most controversial comments came in January of 2004 when he said that most people who wear visors – which he views as cowardly – are "Europeans and French guys." The comment prompted heavy criticism from Quebec and an investigation by Canada's Official Language Commissioner, and caused CBC to impose a seven-second delay on Coach's Corner to allow the network to edit out any remarks it deemed questionable (the delay was eliminated the following season).

On the ice, there have been numerous incidents that have cast the game in a bad light. Marty McSorley on Donald Brashear and Todd Bertuzzi on Steve Moore come to mind as two recent examples of the stick fights, bench-clearing brawls and dirty hits that have long pockmarked hockey and resulted in unwanted media attention and public outcry.

One of the NHL's earliest episodes – which nearly had dire consequences – occurred in Boston on Dec. 13, 1933, when Eddie Shore ended the career of Toronto Maple Leafs star Ace Bailey. Shore charged Bailey from behind, causing him to fall, and Bailey was knocked unconscious and went into convulsions after he hit his head on the ice. In retaliation, Leafs tough guy Red Horner punched Shore, whose head also hit the ice as he fell from the blow. Shore was knocked out and required seven stitches, but wasn't seriously injured. Bailey, meanwhile, was rushed to hospital in critical condition with a fractured skull. He was operated on for more than four hours and there were fears he could die. Shore apologized to Bailey afterwards, but this remains one of the worst on-ice incidents of all-time.

In the 1969 pre-season, Ted Green of the Boston Bruins and Wayne Maki of the St. Louis Blues were involved in a vicious stick-swinging duel. Maki hit Green over the head and Green nearly died of his injuries. He needed three surgeries, missed the next season and had a metal plate inserted in his skull.

There have also been some off-ice controversies involving league executives and team owners.

Former NHL president Gil Stein turned down his induction into the Hall of Fame after it was revealed he rigged the process in order to assure his place in the Hall.

The Pittsburgh Penguins admitted, years after the fact, to essentially tanking the end of the 1984 regular season in order to finish last in the standings and assure themselves the first pick in the draft, Mario Lemieux. That was the impetus for the (some say still flawed) draft lottery the NHL employs today.

Perhaps the most famous case of all is that of former NHLPA boss Alan Eagleson. Eagleson, a driving force behind the 1972 Summit Series, was disgraced when it was discovered he misused union money as well as colluded with NHL team owners to keep salaries down. After being found guilty of charges ranging from mail fraud to racketeering to embezzlement, Eagleson was removed from both the Hall of Fame and the Order of Canada, disbarred as a lawyer, forced to pay six-figure fines and serve six months of an 18-month prison sentence.

Memorable ●●●
Shootout Goals

1. Peter Forsberg's "stamp goal" in the gold medal game at the 1994 Olympics

2. Marek Malik's between-the-legs deke in 15th round of shootout versus Washington in 2005

3. Robert Reichel beats Canada for Czechs at 1998 Olympics

4. Sidney Crosby's water-bottle shot in his first game at Montreal in 2005

5. Jussi Jokinen's stamp goal fake-out

6. Steven Stamkos' behind-both-legs move at 2007 OHL All-Star Game skills competition

7. Pierre-Marc Bouchard's spin-o-rama

8. Rob Schremp's lacrosse-style goal in the 2006 AHL All-Star Game skills competition

9. Pavel Datsyuk's pull-back dangle against Nashville in 2006

10. Jonathan Toews' shootout hat trick for Canada vs. U.S. in 2007 world junior semifinal

It may not be universally loved, but the shootout has provided some of the most jaw-dropping moments in recent hockey history. In fact, Peter Forsberg's move to beat Canada for the gold medal at the 1994 Olympics was so huge, Sweden turned the image into a postage stamp. Likewise, Robert Reichel will always be a hero in the Czech Republic for tallying the only goal in his country's shootout win over Canada in the semifinals at the '98 Games.

Skills competitions at all-star games also provide a good showcase, as there is less at stake – other than bragging rights, which is why Rob Schremp will go down in history for picking up the puck lacrosse-style and whipping it in for a goal at the AHL All-Star Game in 2006.

And of course, some NHL goals just stand out for their timing and innovation. Jussi Jokinen has broken many a goalie's heart by faking Foppa's stamp move before going to his forehand, while Pierre-Marc Bouchard's spin-o-rama came against the Blackhawks and their coach, Denis Savard – who was known to pull the move in games back when he was a player.

But when the Rangers' 6 foot-6 defensive defenseman Marek Malik skated to center ice as the 30th shooter of the night against Washington on Nov. 26, 2005, no one would have predicted he would score on the most memorable maneuver in NHL history, but that's why we watch, isn't it?

Peter
Forsberg

All-Time ● ● ● ●
People Of Power
And Influence

1. CLARENCE CAMPBELL
NHL referee 1933-39; NHL president 1946-77; steered league through first modern expansions and WHA era; Stanley Cup trustee 1979-84.

2. ALAN EAGLESON
First NHLPA director, 1967-91; first big-time player agent; Summit Series promoter; ultimately disgraced and disbarred from law society after being found guilty of embezzling union pension and disability funds and colluding with owners to keep salaries down; sent to prison; lost his Order of Canada and expelled from Hall of Fame.

3. GARY BETTMAN
NHL commissioner 1992-present; oversaw massive league expansion and franchise relocations, and labor disputes in 1994-95 and 2004-05, and Olympic participation.

4. FRANK CALDER
First NHL president 1917-43; helped guide NHL through two World Wars and Great Depression; spearheaded expansion into U.S. and formation of Bruins, Rangers, Red Wings and Blackhawks franchises.

5. BOB GOODENOW
NHLPA director 1992-2005; presided over union during labor disputes in 1994-95 and 2004-05, expansion and relocations, Olympic participation; oversaw explosion in player salaries.

6. WAYNE GRETZKY
Hockey's ultimate ambassador is recognized around the world; highest-scoring player of all-time holds or shares 61 NHL records; demigod status in Canada.

7. BILL WIRTZ

Joined Blackhawks executive in 1952; Chicago Blackhawks
president 1966-2007; helped with NHL and WHA merger;
expansion proponent; involved with first CBA.

8. MAURICE RICHARD

Legendary Canadien and Canadian; an icon of Quebecois culture
and model for "Canadian hockey."

9. KEN LINSEMAN

Directly responsible for getting players under 20 years old
into professional hockey.

10. J. AMBROSE O'BRIEN

Early builder of pro game; founder of the National Hockey Association,
which later became the NHL, and the Montreal Canadiens; played a
huge role in stabilizing the pro game.

Over the past decade, THN has been publishing our annual "100 People of Power and Influence" issue. During that time, the usual suspects – NHL and NHLPA executives, owners, GMs and Wayne Gretzky – have dominated the rankings.

NHL commissioner Gary Bettman topped the list in each of the first eight issues before finally being supplanted by Sidney Crosby in 2008. Former NHLPA director Bob Goodenow placed second to his nemesis Bettman each year until his ouster from the union in 2005. And Gretzky has cracked the top three seven times and has never fallen below sixth.

The all-time list above doesn't stray far from the formula, featuring four NHL commissioners/presidents/founder, two NHLPA directors, an owner, Gretzky and two other former NHL players.

One of those players, Ken Linseman, may elicit a "Huh?" from many people. 'The Rat,' as he was known during his playing days, was a pretty effective player. He potted 20-plus goals seven times, scored the Cup-winning goal for Edmonton in 1984 and was one of the most effective agitators in league history. But it's not Linseman's on-ice exploits that get him included on the all-time list; it's the off-ice maneuvering he made to jump-start his pro career.

In the history of labor relations in professional sport, Linseman was to the NHL what Curt Flood was to Major League Baseball. Linseman didn't challenge free agency rules like Flood did, but he challenged professional hockey's draft rules and forever changed the game.

Today, aspiring NHLers can be drafted when they're 18 years old. But until the late 1970s, players couldn't be drafted or play professionally until they were 20. The Canadian Amateur Hockey Association mandated that players had to stay in junior until the age of 20 and, although not obligated to the CAHA, the NHL and WHA abided by its wishes. So, players under 20 were forced to remain in junior, earning about $50 a week. And that was Linseman's beef.

Ken
Linseman

In 1977, Linseman challenged the NHL's 20-year-old age minimum. The case went to court in Canada, but was dropped after the WHA's Birmingham Bulls drafted and signed the 18-year-old. Trying to stay in CAHA's good books, the WHA attempted to stop the Bulls from signing the youngster, but the Linseman family secured an injunction against the WHA. The ruling was straightforward: Linseman was an adult and should be allowed to earn a living.

It is no surprise Birmingham was the first to challenge the CAHA and raid the junior ranks for players. Renegade Bulls owner John Bassett was concerned only for the health of his franchise and the product on the ice.

"I don't really care what junior hockey thinks," said Bassett to THN in 1978. "I will continue to sign good, underage talent until the laws of junior hockey start conforming with the laws of Canada. I've said it over and over again, but 18-year-olds are allowed to vote and drink and they go to jail. I don't understand why they can't play hockey."

The Linseman ruling opened the floodgates for junior-aged professional players. With the competition for talent between the NHL and the WHA so fierce, other WHA teams began signing underage players – the most famous being the Indianapolis Racers inking Wayne Gretzky at 17 – to the point where the league even stopped holding an amateur draft.

Within two years of the Linseman ruling, the NHL lowered its eligibility age to 18, paving the way for teenage sensations and, some say, turning the draft into more of a crapshoot.

Best Slapshots ● ● ●

1. AL MACINNIS
Won seven of first 10 hardest shot competitions.

2. BOBBY HULL
Caused goalies to ponder career changes.

3. DOUG WILSON
39 goals in 1981-82 for Hawks defender.

4. AL IAFRATE
Won first hardest shot competition and two more after that.

5. BERNIE 'BOOM BOOM' GEOFFRION
His blast popularized use of the slapshot.

6. ANDY BATHGATE
His slapper to Jacques Plante's face prompted the goalie to put on a mask for good.

7. FRANK MAHOVLICH
'The Big M' was lethal when he let it go with a full head of steam down the wing.

8. DENIS POTVIN
Mike Bossy from the slot, Potvin from the point.

9. TIM HORTON
Strong as an ox, he put everything into his big shot.

10. CHRIS PRONGER
Always low, hard and right on target.

Mike Liut became a player agent after a 13-year NHL career. But had the St. Louis Blues goalie taken a few more Al MacInnis drives off the noggin during his days in the crease, he might have begun negotiating other players' contracts a lot sooner.

A 20-year-old MacInnis once wired a puck off Liut's mask that knocked the goalie over on its way into the net. Shortly thereafter, Liut began musing about career changes.

"If (getting hit) happens too often, you have to sit down and re-evaluate what you're doing with your life," Liut once said of being nailed by MacInnis' famous slapper.

MacInnis, a defenseman who piled up power play points, won the NHL's hardest shot contest seven times in the first 10 years of the competition, always using his trusty wooden stick rather than a composite model.

Montreal Canadiens legend Bernie Geoffrion is often credited with inventing the slapshot in the 1950s, prompting longtime hockey observer Stan Fischler to write that 'Boom Boom' was to shooting pucks what gunpowder was to warfare.

Geoffrion said he was awakened to the power of whacking the puck after he swatted at one in anger during practice and noticed how it took off.

The genesis of the slapper, in truth, may have come some time before Geoffrion. Archie Wilcox played in the NHL during the 1930s and in an interview after his playing days in the early '40s, Wilcox referenced something he called a "bat" shot. He said a former player and old coach of his, Jimmy Gardiner, preached using this technique when shooters were within 10 feet

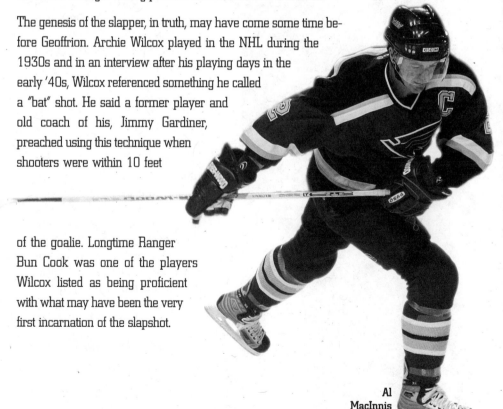

of the goalie. Longtime Ranger Bun Cook was one of the players Wilcox listed as being proficient with what may have been the very first incarnation of the slapshot.

Al
MacInnis

Things Thrown
On The Ice

1. HATS

It began in the 1950s with the New York Rangers' minor league affiliate in Guelph, Ont., which was nicknamed the Mad Hatters. The owner had a tradition of giving a hat to any player who scored three goals in a game. Sammy Taft, who owned a hat shop in Toronto, offered the same prize for any Maple Leaf who achieved the feat. Fans caught on and began throwing hats onto the ice after a player's third goal of the game and the tradition has stuck to this day.

Al Sabotka

2. OCTOPUS

The practise started in Detroit in 1952 as a symbol of the number of playoff games needed to win the Stanley Cup in the pre-expansion era: one tentacle for every victory.

3. RATS

A tradition that infested Southern Florida during the Panthers' run to the 1996 Stanley Cup final. At the start of the season, winger Scott Mellanby killed a rat in the dressing room and then scored two goals that night using the same stick. Word got out about Mellanby's "rat trick" and Florida fans littered the ice with plastic rats after big goals and throughout the playoffs.

4. STUFFED ANIMALS

This is more common in minor hockey. Fans are encouraged to bring stuffed animals to the rink and throw them on the ice after the first goal. The animals are then collected and given away to charity. It was taken to a new level in Portland on Nov. 24, 2007, when 6,343 fans threw a record 20,372 stuffed animals onto the ice after the first goal of the game. The best part? The goal was disallowed.

5. BEER BOTTLES

Usually thrown after the visiting team scores, in overtime, or after a disputed penalty call. Jeff Carter experienced this while doing a post-game interview after his Flyers defeated the Capitals in overtime of Game 7 in their 2008 first round playoff series. Luckily for Carter, the bottle that whizzed by his head was plastic.

6. PROSTHETIC LEG

This incident allegedly took place at a Corpus Christi Icerays (CHL) game in the 1990s. A fan sitting near the glass became so disgruntled with the refereeing, he took off his prosthetic leg and threw it onto the ice. One does wonder, though, how did he get home?

7. BENCH

On Jan. 30, 2000, New Jersey Devils coach Robbie Ftorek got so upset at a non-call that he picked up the team's wooden bench and chucked it onto the ice. He was suspended one game and fined $10,000.

8. DEAD GOPHERS

An old University of North Dakota tradition. Fans would take frozen, dead gophers (how they got them is beyond us) and toss them onto the ice after goals when UND played the University of Minnesota Golden Gophers.

9. FISH

An Alaska Aces (ECHL) tradition. Fans traditionally throw frozen fish (usually salmon) onto the ice after a goal.

10. PUCKS

One example of why giveaway nights should be held with bated breath. During the 1972 home opener of the short-lived Philadelphia Blazers franchise in the WHA, fans were handed orange pucks before the game. Unfortunately, before game time, the Zamboni broke through the ice, causing the game to be cancelled. Fans began tossing the pucks onto the surface, scaring away the officials who were trying to calm things down.

Most Memorable ● ● ●
TV/Radio Calls

1. "He shoots, he scores!" – FOSTER HEWITT
The definitive hockey call.

2. "Here's a shot! Henderson made a wild stab for it and fell. Here's another shot! Right in front, they score! Henderson has scored for Canada!" – FOSTER HEWITT
Paul Henderson scores the winning goal late in Game 8 of the 1972 Summit Series.

3. "Do you believe in miracles?...Yes! Unbelievable!" – AL MICHAELS
The U.S. defeats the Soviet Union 4-3 in the medal round of the 1980 Olympics at Lake Placid, N.Y.

4. "Bobby Orr...behind the net to Sanderson to Orr! Bobby Orr! Bobby Orr scores and the Boston Bruins have won the Stanley Cup!" – DAN KELLY
Bobby Orr's iconic goal wins the Stanley Cup for Boston in 1970.

5. "Spinarama," "Scintillating save," "Paraphernalia," "Cannonading shot." – DANNY GALLIVAN
Longtime CBC announcer entertained viewers and annoyed English professors with his homegrown words.

6. "May Day! May Day! May Day! May Day! May Day! May Day!" – RICK JEANNERET
Buffalo's Brad May scores overtime winner against Boston in Game 4 of 1993 Adams Division semifinal.

7. "Gretzky, looking, Jari Kurri, McSorley, to Gretzkyyyyy, scooores, he did it! He did it! The greatest goal-scorer in National Hockey League history is Wayne Gretzky!" – GARY THORNE
Wayne Gretzky scores the 802nd goal of his NHL career on March 23, 1994, to pass Gordie Howe for most all-time.

8. "They're goin' home, they're goin' home. Yeah, they're goin' home!" – BOB COLE

The Soviet Union's Central Red Army team leaves the ice mid-game during a Jan. 11, 1976, exhibition match against the Philadelphia Flyers.

9. "Oh, the Penguins have won the Stanley Cup! Oh Lord Stanley, Lord Stanley, get me the brandy!" – MIKE LANGE

Pittsburgh beats Chicago in 1992 for the Penguins' second consecutive Cup.

10. "Salt Lake City, 2002, men's ice hockey, gold medal, Canada!" – BOB COLE

As the seconds ticked down on Canada's first Olympic gold medal in men's hockey in 50 years.

"Hello, Canada, and hockey fans in the United States and Newfoundland." Beginning in the 1920s, that was Foster Hewitt's weekly greeting at the start of radio and, later, TV broadcasts of *Hockey Night In Canada*. Hewitt, the voice of *HNIC* for 40 years, practically invented many of the phrases that announcers still use today to describe the action.

Of course, some of hockey's current play-by-play men have added their own personal touches. Pittsburgh Penguins announcer Mike Lange has come up with "Scratch my back with a hacksaw!" and "Buy Sam a drink and get his dog one, too!" among his many gems. The phrases might not make a lot

Al Michaels

of sense, yet they effectively convey Lange's amazement at the exploits of Mario Lemieux, Jaromir Jagr and Sidney Crosby. In Buffalo, Rick Jeanneret also has had a lot of highlight-reel calls, including "La-La-La-La-La-La-LaFontaine!" and "Stuu-uuuuuuuuuu Barnes! Up on the top shelf where mama hides the coooookiesssssss!" But his "May Day!" call is by far the most memorable of them all. Jeanneret once said there was no way for him to predetermine the call that ended that game: "Brad May hadn't scored in about 13 games at that point…I just kept saying 'May Day!' over and over until I could think of something else to say."

But back to Hewitt and hockey's all-time most memorable phrase. Repeated at games at nearly every level of play, "He shoots, he scores!" is as shinny as it gets. Uttered for the first time on March 21, 1923, during his first live hockey broadcast, those four words have cemented Hewitt's legacy. The phrase has been used by kids playing ball hockey on the street before dinner, grown men in late-night beer leagues and professional broadcasters in Game 7 playoff overtimes.

Foster Hewitt

Definitive ● ● ● ●
Sounds Of The Game

1. Skate blade cutting into the ice
2. Horn and crowd noise after a goal
3. Slapshot
4. Puck hitting the post
5. Play-by-play of an overtime goal in the playoffs
6. Crash of bodies against the boards
7. A hard tape-to-tape pass being cleanly accepted
8. Referee's whistle
9. Organ music
10. Bag of pucks being dropped onto the ice

Hockey is a full sensory experience. From the touch of the pads against your skin, to the sight of teammates celebrating a game-winning goal, to the smell of the rink, to the taste of salty sweat on your lips, to the sounds of the game all around you. This list is obviously subjective and can be emotional and personal, too, as each of these sounds might conjure up a specific childhood memory or experience.

More often than not, the first hockey sound people think of is the crisp, clean grind of a skate blade cutting into the ice. There's something mystical about that singular sound. It goes back to our memories of first setting foot on a frozen pond or local rink and learning how to skate. The gratification that comes with being able to take your first steps on slippery ice is something that stays with you forever, and we are reminded of this every time we watch or play hockey, from millionaire NHLers competing for the Stanley Cup to children battling it out for neighborhood bragging rights. All 10 sounds on this list have a story and a context that come with them, and all say something about the game we love so much.

Best ● ● ● ● ●
Power Forwards

1. CAM NEELY
Bruins fans still curse Ulf Samuelsson's name.

2. MARK MESSIER
Six-time Cup winner second in all-time points.

3. JAROME IGINLA
Surname means 'Big Tree' in father's native African language.

4. BRENDAN SHANAHAN
Should be celebrated for play and attempts to better game.

5. ERIC LINDROS
Unstoppable force before concussion problems.

6. KEITH TKACHUK
First American to lead NHL in goals (52 in '96-97).

7. RICK TOCCHET
Known as much for his fisticuffs, Stanley Cup
winner had 440 career goals.

8. KEVIN STEVENS
Two-time NHL all-star and U.S. Olympian also won two Cups.

9. JOHN LECLAIR
'Legion of Doom' member had back-to-back-to-back 50-goal campaigns.

10. TIM KERR
Hard to believe this four-time 50-goal man went undrafted.

While players from years gone by – from Gordie Howe and Bobby Hull to Terry O'Reilly and Clark Gillies – have displayed the hard-nosed style that typifies the power forward position, this list is reserved for the men who skated during or after the label entered hockey's vernacular.

And the definition of a power forward was born with Boston Bruins brawler-sniper Cam Neely. In the late 1980s and early '90s, the right winger ruled the NHL as a physical force who was a devastating bodychecker, feared fighter and skilled scorer. One of only nine NHLers to score 50 goals in 50 games – needing only 44 injury-plagued games in 1993-94 – Neely was inducted into the Hall of Fame in 2005.

But what of The Moose? Mark Messier was a better overall player than Neely, but his days as a true power forward, while dominant, were limited to early in his career. Messier played some left wing on a line with Wayne Gretzky with the Oilers in the early '80s – power forwards have traditionally been defined as wingers, as opposed to centers, because wingers usually have more opportunity to bodycheck and be physical – but spent most of his career as a center.

Cam
Neely

Most •••••
Significant
Rule Changes

1. FORWARD PASSING IS ALLOWED IN DEFENDING AND NEUTRAL ZONES IN 1927-28

Extended in 1929-30 to include all three zones, but not across blueline.

2. GOALIES PERMITTED TO FALL TO THE ICE TO MAKE SAVES IN 1917-18

Previously, a goaltender was penalized for dropping to the ice.

3. INTRODUCTION OF TWO LINES PAINTED ON THE ICE IN 1918-19

Lines added 20 feet on each side of center, creating three playing zones and a 40-foot neutral zone where forward passing was permitted. Prior to the addition of the lines, players could only pass laterally or backwards.

4. RED LINE AT CENTER INTRODUCED TO SPEED UP THE GAME AND REDUCE OFFSIDE CALLS IN 1943-44

The modern era begins.

5. PLAYER SERVING A MINOR PENALTY ALLOWED TO RETURN TO THE ICE WHEN A GOAL IS SCORED BY OPPOSING TEAM IN 1956-57

Thank the high-scoring Habs for this change; previously, penalized players had to sit in the box for the full two minutes.

6. ONE REFEREE AND TWO LINESMEN TO OFFICIATE GAMES IN 1941-42

Originally there were two refs, then one ref and one linesman; the one-ref-two-linesmen combo lasted 60 years until another ref was added.

7. WEARING OF HELMETS MADE MANDATORY FOR PLAYERS ENTERING THE NHL IN 1979-80

Craig MacTavish never got the memo on this one.

8. FIVE-MINUTE SUDDEN-DEATH OVERTIME TO BE PLAYED IN REGULAR SEASON GAMES THAT ARE TIED AT THE END OF REGULATION TIME IN 1983-84

What?! Overtime during the regular season?! What's next?! Shootouts?! (Yes...introduced in 2005-06.)

9. VIDEO REPLAY IS INTRODUCED TO HELP REFEREES IN GOAL/NO GOAL SITUATIONS IN 1991-92

And there was never another argument again about whether or not "that goal should have counted"...

10. CENTER RED LINE ELIMINATED FOR TWO-LINE PASSES IN 2005-06

It doesn't lead to breakaway after breakaway, but it opens things up a bit.

In its 90-plus years of existence, the NHL has changed its rules many times. No change was more influential than allowing the forward pass. Prior to the 1927-28 season, hockey looked like rugby on ice as only backward passes were permitted. For two seasons, the forward pass was only allowed in the defending and neutral zones; in 1929-30, the rule was extended to include all zones.

These days, goalies sometimes complain about restrictions on the size of their equipment, but prior to 1917 every goaltender was forced to employ a stand-up style as falling to the ice to make a save was forbidden. With so many current netminders using the butterfly style, it's hard to imagine how any saves were made when goalies couldn't drop down. Of course, the fact goalies during this time didn't wear a helmet or a mask might have provided some motivation to stay on their feet.

Finally, while Sean Avery's on-ice antics led to a re-interpretation of the rule regarding goaltender interference in the middle of the 2008 playoffs, no team has ever forced the hand of the NHL's lawmakers like the Montreal Canadiens of the 1950s. Their power play was so strong they would often score multiple times on a single penalty. This forced the NHL to change the rule to allow a penalized player to return to the ice once a goal was scored. It didn't slow down the Habs much, though; they still won five straight Stanley Cups.

Mario Lemieux

Best
Players By Country
Canada

1. WAYNE GRETZKY
No. 99 is No. 1

2. BOBBY ORR
Revolutionized the defense position

3. GORDIE HOWE
The perfect hockey prototype

4. MARIO LEMIEUX
Saved the Penguins franchise in the '80s...and '90s...and 21st century

5. MAURICE RICHARD
'The Rocket' was the first to score 50 goals in a season

6. DOUG HARVEY
Two-way defender won seven Norris Trophies and six Stanley Cups

7. JEAN BELIVEAU
One of the classiest men to ever lace up skates

8. BOBBY HULL
Built to skate and score

9. PATRICK ROY
Winningest goalie in NHL history

10. EDDIE SHORE
Only defenseman to win Hart Trophy four times

Jaromir Jagr

Czech Republic
(including Czechoslovakia)

1. JAROMIR JAGR
Five-time NHL scoring champion first Czech to surpass 600 NHL goals

2. DOMINIK HASEK
Six-time Vezina Trophy winner copped two Stanley Cups in Detroit

3. PETER STASTNY*
Only Wayne Gretzky had more points in the 1980s

4. PETER BONDRA*
Scored 503 goals in 1,081 NHL games

5. VACLAV NEDOMANSKY
Powerful skater with heavy wrist shot scored 163 goals
in 220 international matches

6. VLADIMIR MARTINEC
Pure finesse player was almost impossible to stop 1-on-1

7. FRANTISEK POSPISIL
Cool-headed national team captain led country to three
world championships in 1970s

8. JAN SUCHY
Dimunitive defender, in mode of Pierre Pilote, acted as
second goalie with fearless shot-blocking

9. IVAN HLINKA
National team captain with huge desire was unstoppable
once he reached top speed

10. ZIGGY PALFFY*
Averaged more than a point per game in 684 NHL contests

*Slovak players

Teemu Selanne

Finland

1. JARI KURRI
Highest-scoring Finn in NHL history (601 goals and 1,398 points)
won five Stanley Cups with Edmonton

2. TEEMU SELANNE
Second Finn to score 500 NHL goals

3. SAKU KOIVU
Habs captain won courageous battle with cancer

4. JERE LEHTINEN
Three-time Selke Trophy winner helped Dallas win only Cup in 1999

5. ESA TIKKANEN
Feisty winger was playoff star with 132 points in 186 NHL post-season games

6. MIIKKA KIPRUSOFF
Best Finnish goalie of all-time was Vezina Trophy winner in 2006

7. TEPPO NUMMINEN
Has played more NHL games (1,315) than any other European

8. RAIMO HELMINEN
Played more international games for his country (331)
than any player from any country

9. REIJO RUOTSALAINEN
Highly skilled offensive blueliner recorded 344 points in 446 NHL
games with the Rangers, Edmonton and New Jersey

10. PETTERI NUMMELIN
Has played in 13 world championships, more than any other Finnish defenseman

Vladislav Tretiak

Russia
(including Soviet Union)

1. SLAVA FETISOV
Soul of the Soviet national team in the 1980s won two
Stanley Cups with Detroit

2. VLADISLAV TRETIAK
Summit Series star won four Olympic gold medals

3. SERGEI MAKAROV
Won Soviet Elite League scoring title nine times

4. VALERY KHARLAMOV
Brilliant stickhandler sparkled in 1972 Summit Series

5. ANATOLI FIRSOV
Lightning-quick thinker invented new techniques like dropping
the puck back to his skates to fool a defender

6. PAVEL BURE
Dynamic winger scored more than 50 goals five times

7. SERGEI FEDOROV
Three-time Stanley Cup champ has more NHL points (1,156)
than any other Russian player

8. ALEXANDER MOGILNY
First Soviet player to defect has more NHL goals (473)
than any other Russian player

9. ALEXEI KOVALEV
Wayne Gretzky once called him the most highly skilled player in NHL

10. IGOR LARIONOV
Three-time Stanley Cup winner selected for Hall of Fame in 2008

Mats Sundin

Sweden

1. NICKLAS LIDSTROM
Best Swedish defender of all-time has won six Norris Trophies

2. PETER FORSBERG
Once considered the NHL's best two-way player

3. SVEN 'TUMBA' JOHANSSON
Named Sweden's best player of the 20th century, he introduced
the slapshot to his country

4. BORJE SALMING
Pioneer in early 1970s destroyed the image of 'chicken Swede'

5. MATS SUNDIN
He has 555 goals in 1,305 NHL games, more than any other
Swedish player in both categories

6. ANDERS HEDBERG
Speedy winger was a huge star in WHA before signing with
the Rangers late in his career

7. LENNART SVEDBERG
Star defenseman in 1960s, nicknamed 'Lille Stramma' ("the little streak")
due to his great speed

8. THOMAS STEEN
Only Swedish player to have his jersey retired by an NHL club

9. KENT NILSSON
Nicknamed 'Magic Man' because of great skills, he averaged 1.2 points
per game in 553 NHL contests

10. DANIEL ALFREDSSON
Ottawa captain has scored 331 NHL goals

Mike Modano

United States

1. MIKE MODANO
All-time leader in goals and points among American-born players

2. CHRIS CHELIOS
Won his third Cup at age 46

3. BRIAN LEETCH
Smooth D-man piled up 1,000 points in 18 NHL seasons

4. JEREMY ROENICK
Three 100-plus point seasons for passionate star

5. MIKE RICHTER
Recorded 300 career wins, all with the Rangers

6. TOM BARRASSO
Backstopped the Penguins to their only two Stanley Cups

7. PHIL HOUSLEY
All-time leader in points among American defensemen

8. PAT LAFONTAINE
Stellar career was cut short due to injuries

9. JOE MULLEN
First American-born player to score 500 goals

10. NEAL BROTEN
Won titles in NCAA, Olympics and NHL

Players Who Left ● ● The NHL Too Early

1. BOBBY ORR
Eight Norris Trophies, three Harts, two Conn Smythes;
injuries force him to retire at 30.

2. MIKE BOSSY
Averages 57 goals for 10 seasons; injuries force him to retire at 30.

3. KEN DRYDEN
Five Vezinas and six Stanley Cups in eight seasons; retires at 32.

4. BILL DURNAN
Six Vezinas in seven-year career; retires at 35.

5. PELLE LINDBERGH
First-team all-star and Vezina winner in 1985;
dies in car accident in November of 1986.

6. VLADIMIR KONSTANTINOV
Plus-60 rating and second-team all-star in 1995-96; won the Cup and was a
Norris nominee in 1996-97; severely injured in limo accident in summer of '97.

7. BILL BARILKO
Four Cups in five seasons; dies in a plane crash at 24.

8. BILL MASTERTON
Only NHL player to die due to an on-ice incident.

9. NORMAND LEVEILLE
14th pick in 1981 draft, 42 points in 75 games before being forced to
retire due to a brain aneurysm at 19.

10. NEWSY LALONDE
One of Montreal Canadiens' original 'Flying Frenchmen,' sold to rival
league after feuding with management.

There have been many players who've left the NHL before their time. Two World Wars, the Great Depression and lower salaries in the league's early decades have forced unwanted retirement upon many. But the players listed here made the list for other reasons as well, such as business, injury, tragedy and other perplexing factors.

NHL fans know the Bill Masterton Memorial Trophy as the annual award for the player who displays "perseverance, sportsmanship and dedication to hockey," but Masterton himself is somewhat unknown.

Masterton grew up in Winnipeg and was a college hockey star at the University of Denver for a Pioneers team that won three NCAA championships in four years. He earned a four-year degree in engineering at Denver and was named MVP of the 1961 NCAA tournament.

After Denver, Masterton earned a master's degree in finance and played minor pro for two years. He retired to the business world, playing semi-pro senior hockey and for the U.S. national team in his spare time until 1967, when expansion doubled the number of NHL jobs. Masterton's rights were traded to the Minnesota North Stars and he began living his dream.

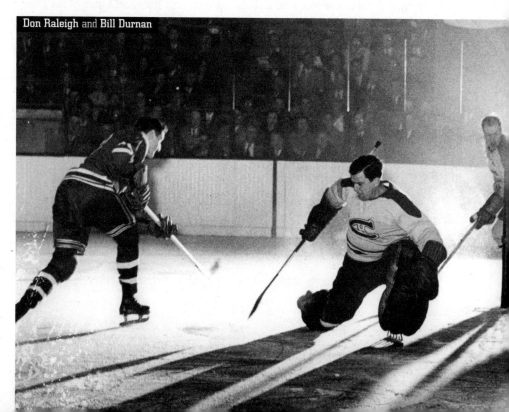

Don Raleigh and Bill Durnan

Bill Durnan

But tragedy struck during his 38th NHL game when Masterton was checked and fell awkwardly to the ice, hitting his head. He suffered a brain hemorrhage so severe doctors were unable to operate, and died two days later. The accident buoyed the mandatory helmet movement and the rule was grandfathered in at the beginning of the 1979-80 NHL season.

At the other end of the spectrum, if a Bill Durnan Trophy were to be awarded, it would go to players who retired at the top of their game.

In the 1930s and early '40s, Durnan played senior hockey, backstopping the Kirkland Lake (Ont.) Blue Devils to the Allan Cup in 1940 before moving to the Quebec Senior League to play for the Montreal Royals. Success with the Royals caught the attention of the Montreal Canadiens, who decided on Durnan as their starter for the 1943-44 season. But the enigmatic goalie held out for a larger contract, preferring the amateur game to the pressure of the pros if the money wasn't right.

On opening night, Durnan remained unsigned. Legend has it 10 minutes before the game, the Habs finally relented to the goalie's demands. Durnan played and went on to lead the NHL in games played, wins and goals-against average that season. Montreal won its first Stanley Cup in 13 seasons and Durnan became the first rookie netminder to win the Vezina Trophy.

The ambidextrous Durnan was the last goalie to captain an NHL team. He won the Vezina his first four seasons in the NHL and six times overall, led the NHL in wins four times and goals-against average six times, earned first-team all-star honors six times and won two Cups. But Durnan retired suddenly after his seventh season, while still at the top of his game, saying he'd lost the desire to continue playing.

Worst Helmets ● ● ● ●

Butch Goring

1. **BUTCH GORING**
2. **MIKE FOLIGNO**
3. **PETR KLIMA**
4. **STAN MIKITA**
5. **RICHIE DUNN**
6. **MATS SUNDIN**
7. **WAYNE GRETZKY**
8. **RICK VAIVE**
9. **GILBERT PERREAULT**
10. **ULF SAMUELSSON**

We can thank designers at Jofa for producing some of the ugliest helmets in hockey history. Butch Goring got his first Jofa when he was 12 years old and wore it for his entire NHL career. Every time he was traded he simply painted his beloved helmet the color of his new team. While Goring was one of the first NHL players to wear a helmet regularly, what he wore on his head didn't offer much protection; by today's standards, it wouldn't even be certified.

Another victim of Jofa's helmet designs was Petr Klima, whose garbage pail helmet was memorably bad. Klima, though, wasn't alone. Over a 10-year span from the mid-'80s to the early '90s, a large group of NHLers bought into the bubble helmet look, including Mario Lemieux, Jaromir Jagr and Pat Verbeek.

Best Puckhandling ●● Goalies

1. MARTIN BRODEUR
Head and shoulders better than his generation, inspired followers.

2. RON HEXTALL
First goalie to shoot the puck and score a goal.

3. MARTY TURCO
Ability to go from glove to stick to pass is impeccable.

4. RICK DIPIETRO
Gradual development forgiven by effectiveness with the puck.

5. TOM BARRASSO
Good enough for Scotty Bowman to draft him No. 5 overall.

6. ED BELFOUR
Not always pretty, but usually effective.

7. GARY SMITH
He's the reason why goalies can't pass red line.

8. ED GIACOMIN
First goalie to record two assists in a game – and he hit a post.

9. GERRY CHEEVERS
Played forward for a season in junior.

10. JACQUES PLANTE
Father of the mask known to wander.

The importance of a good puckhandling goalie hasn't been a big part of the NHL for the past few years, but it has roots as far back as Jacques Plante, who would occasionally roam well out of his crease. But comparing the goalies of today to those of yesteryear is like night and day. Today, the style is practised and perfected, but in the time of Gerry Cheevers, Ed Giacomin and Gary 'Suitcase' Smith, it was much more improvised. However, those tenders still deserve recognition for starring in their time.

Smith inspired the NHL to create a rule restricting goalies from crossing the center red line after he carried the puck up ice. Giacomin is recognized by Glenn 'Chico' Resch and John Davidson as being the first to truly incorporate roving into his game, while Cheevers – who played a little forward in junior – is also considered among the best of his era.

Ron Hextall and Tom Barrasso bridged the gap from the pioneers to the perfectionists; Hextall became the first goalie to shoot the puck and score a goal, both in the regular season and post-season. Modern goalies became so effective, the league in 2005-06 introduced the trapezoid area behind the nets where goalies aren't allowed to play the puck.

Ron Hextall

Best ●●●●●●
Backhand Shots

1. MAURICE RICHARD
2. GORDIE HOWE
3. MATS SUNDIN
4. ANDY BATHGATE
5. SYL APPS
6. DAVE KEON
7. SIDNEY CROSBY
8. RED BERENSON
9. MILT SCHMIDT
10. WAYNE GRETZKY

When it comes to guiding pucks into nets, deception can be as useful as velocity.

Just ask any goaltender who has been beaten by a backhand.

Though it was a much more viable option when players were using straight blades, the backhand maintains a place in the game today. Anybody who has seen a Toronto Maple Leafs game in the past 15 years can likely envision the right-shooting Mats Sundin barreling in on a goalie, pulling the puck to his backhand and chipping a piece of paint off the bottom of the crossbar en route to a goal.

The backhand is a very effective weapon from in close. Sundin, for instance, uses it to quickly change the angle and elevate the puck. Maurice Richard, who drove to the net with more jam than any player in hockey history, used the backside of the blade to jam pucks over the line as he darted through the crease.

But even from 10 feet out, the backhand's deceptive nature can make catching it a handful for goalies.

Even Mr. Goalie.

"The backhand, it was more difficult to tell if it was high or low than the forehand," said Hall of Fame netminder Glenn Hall.

Another layer of confusion is created by the actual shooting motion involved with a backhand.

"They used to follow through," Hall noted. "And so the stick was a problem too, and they used to follow through on the backhand more than on the forehand."

Gordie Howe

Best Playmakers Since Expansion

1. WAYNE GRETZKY (1.32 assists per game)
Recorded more assists than the NHL's second-leading scorer had points four times in his career.

2. MARIO LEMIEUX (1.13 assists per game)
Turned journeymen Warren Young and Rob Brown into 40-goal scorers.

3. BOBBY ORR (0.98 assists per game)
First NHLer to crack the 100-assist mark in a single season.

4. ADAM OATES (0.81 assists per game)
Hull and Oates made sweet music together.

5. PETER FORSBERG (0.90 assists per game)
Had 13 assists in nine games in 2007-08 playing on one foot.

6. STEVE YZERMAN (0.81 assists per game)
Even when he became a defensive forward, he could still thread the needle.

7. PETER STASTNY (0.81 assists per game)
Helped push Jacques Richard over the 50-goal mark as a rookie.

8. BERNIE FEDERKO (0.76 assists per game)
His 761 assists got him into the Hall of Fame.

9. BOBBY CLARKE (0.74 assists per game)
Having targets such as Reggie Leach and Rick MacLeish sure helped.

10. JOE SAKIC (0.74 assists per game)
Draws defenders to him and then dishes to the open man.

Wayne Gretzky set up **Mario Lemieux's** memorable series winner in the 1987 Canada Cup.

Wayne Gretzky never held down an office job.

But make no mistake about it, the most prolific scorer in NHL history did have an office – it was in every arena he ever played in, located behind the opposition's net. Although Gretzky revolutionized the game in several ways, there are many who will remember him best setting up behind the opposing team's net and working his magic.

The Great One, with his head up and waiting patiently with the puck, befuddled goaltenders and confused defenders. What was he going to do? Pass it in front? Hit one of his defensemen sneaking in from the point? Direct it to a teammate in the slot for a one-timer? Flip it in off the back of the goalie's leg? He had so many options.

Gretzky used the wraparound like a fastball-throwing pitcher incorporates the change-up into his repertoire – a little something to keep goaltenders off-balance.

And when Gretzky wasn't working from his office, he'd often try to hit a trailing teammate after carrying the puck into the opposition's zone and then curling back to consider his options.

All told, Gretzky either led or tied for the NHL lead in assists 16 times in his career, including his first 13 seasons in the league.

Worst Injuries ● ● ●

1. BILL MASTERTON
Strikes his head on the ice after being checked and dies 48 hours later.

2. HOWIE MORENZ
Habs legend suffers a multiple fractured leg and dies of blood clots
while recovering in the hospital.

3. CLINT MALARCHUK
Has his throat slashed by Steve Tuttle's skate in a crease collision,
slicing open his external carotid artery.

4. BRYAN BERARD
Toronto defenseman loses the sight in his right eye after being struck
by Marian Hossa's stick during the follow-through of a shot.

5. RICHARD ZEDNIK
Florida right winger has his throat sliced open by teammate Olli Jokinen's skate.

6. MARK HOWE
Impaled himself on a metal post in the middle of the net
after sliding into it tush-first.

7. GORDIE HOWE
In an attempt to hit Ted Kennedy, Howe misses and flies head-first
into the boards, fracturing his skull. An operation is performed to
relieve pressure on his brain.

8. ACE BAILEY
Develops a brain tumor after engaging in a stick fight with Eddie Shore.

9. TRENT McCLEARY
His career ends prematurely after being hit in the throat by
a Chris Therien slapshot.

10. BORJE SALMING
Cut in the face by Gerard Gallant's skate, Salming receives 300 stitches.

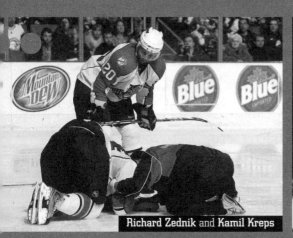

Richard Zednik and Kamil Kreps

Richard Zednik

Poor Ryan Malone.

While playing in the Stanley Cup final last season with the Pittsburgh Penguins, the bruising power forward broke his nose – not once, but twice. The first time was in Game 1 when he ran into a dump truck named Niklas Kronwall. The second time came in Game 5 when his own teammate, defenseman Hal Gill, nailed him in the beak with a slapshot.

By the end of the final, Malone looked like he had just gone five rounds with Mike Tyson. But as beaten and battered as Malone was, he didn't come close to cracking our top 10 list of the NHL's worst injuries.

Injuries are part of the game. Players accept that every time they skate onto the ice. You never know when it will occur, but you can bet your bottom dollar if you play hockey, you will get injured. It could be like Eric Lindros, cutting through the neutral zone when suddenly he was laid out by a Scott Stevens hit. Or it could be something as simple as taking a slapshot off the big toe. Heck, Dave Manson was punched in the throat during a fight and never spoke the same again.

Players are routinely cut, quickly stitched up and sent back into action within minutes of their injury. A baseball pitcher misses a start if he has a blister, but a hockey player breaks his jaw and simply attaches a cage to his helmet.

Greatest ● ● ● ●
NHL Comebacks

1. MARIO LEMIEUX

Start with the Penguins legend's comeback from a bout with cancer in 1993; then, behold his return to the league in 2000, three years after nagging back woes led to his retirement. Much like his superior scoring talents, nobody could match Super Mario's ability to overcome the odds – and look magnificent doing so.

2. PETER FORSBERG

One of the toughest NHL superstars in history, the Swedish native had his spleen removed during the 2001 playoffs and missed the entire '01-02 campaign recovering from multiple injuries. When he returned for the 2002-03 season, he led the league in scoring and was named NHL MVP.

3. GORDIE HOWE

The Red Wings star first retired from the NHL after 25 seasons at age 43. Mr. Hockey took a couple years off and, when he returned to the upstart World Hockey Association, picked up right where he left off, averaging at least 30 goals and 100 points in his first three comeback seasons with the Houston Aeros.

4. GARY ROBERTS

He'd already won a Stanley Cup by the time bone spurs and nerve damage in his neck forced him to the sidelines for the entire 1996-97 season, but Roberts was far from finished. In fact, he's still playing and still scoring and has established himself as one of the most tenacious men to ever play the game.

5. SAKU KOIVU

The Canadiens captain battled cancer and a serious eye injury during his career, and beat them both to remain a central part of his team's success. He also won the 2001-02 Bill Masterton Trophy for dedication to the sport.

6. BRYAN BERARD

A wayward stick left Berard with virtually no vision in his right eye in 2000. But after a season removed from the game, he returned to the NHL in 2001.

Mario Lemieux

7. HOCKEY TO MINNESOTA

When North Stars owner Norm Green moved the NHL franchise to Dallas in 1993, he seriously wounded all hockey fans in one of the sport's grass-roots states. It took the NHL nearly seven years to correct its egregious mistake, but when the expansion Wild took the ice in 2000, the game was back where it belonged.

8. STEVE YZERMAN

A severe knee injury forced the Wings captain into radical reconstructive surgery in 2002, leaving many wondering if he'd ever play again. But he did and enjoyed three more productive seasons in Detroit before retiring in 2006.

9. TED NOLAN

Proving that coaches can overcome distress as well as any player, Nolan returned to an NHL bench in 2006 for the first time in nine years – and for his first season since winning the Jack Adams Award with Buffalo in 1996-97. As bench boss of the Isles, he led his new team to its first playoff berth since 2004.

10. ALEXANDRE DAIGLE

Many expected great things out of Daigle – who was chosen first overall by Ottawa in 1993 – but little was delivered; instead, he spent parts of the 1999-2000 and 2000-01 campaigns in the AHL. But as a member of the Minnesota Wild in 2003-04, Daigle put up a respectable 20-goal, 51-point season that helped salvage at least a little dignity for him.

Best ● ● ● ● ● ●
NHL Cities

1. MONTREAL

It has been suggested that hockey is a religion and not a sport in Montreal. Fans dissect every game, practice and transaction as though their lives depended on it; at the same time, Canadiens fans have more fun at a game than anybody on the planet. Oh yeah, they lead the universe in Stanley Cup celebrations, too.

2. TORONTO

All you need to know about the Leafs is, they have not won the Stanley Cup since 1967 and have not had an unsold seat since Moby Dick was a minnow. Or, as one journalist put it, "If the Leafs played at 3 a.m. during a blinding snowstorm, there wouldn't be an empty seat in the house."

3. EDMONTON

Hold an outdoor game in the dead of winter at an outdoor football stadium? No problem; it's a sell-out. Oilers fans are a special breed. They love their city and they love their team and heaven help anybody that disses either. City of Champions, indeed.

4. CALGARY

Flames followers exposed themselves as some of the most enthusiastic in all of hockey during the 2004 final against Tampa Bay. Truth be told, they've been among the NHL's most loyal and energetic fans since the team arrived in Calgary in 1980.

5. DETROIT

Don't believe the rumors; Hockeytown is alive and thriving. Faced with a declining economy, Red Wings fans still filled Joe Louis Arena in 2008 and were rewarded with a fourth Stanley Cup in 11 seasons.

6. PHILADELPHIA

It has been more than three decades since the Flyers faithful was rewarded with a Stanley Cup, but local interest in the team has never waned. And it all stems from the enthusiastic and loyal ownership of Ed Snider.

Dejected **Calgary** Flames fans walk the "Red Mile" after the Flames were eliminated by the Tampa Bay Lightning in Game 7 of the 2004 Stanley Cup Final.

7. NEW YORK

The Rangers have won one Stanley Cup since 1940 – the magical 1994 run led by Mark Messier – but Madison Square Garden remains a special building that plays host to some of hockey's most raucous supporters.

8. MINNESOTA

It used to be said that Minnesotans love their hockey, they just don't like the NHL. That is no longer the case. While high school and college hockey continue to thrive, the Wild is now the biggest show in the Twin Cities.

9. COLORADO

Call it second time lucky. The Colorado Rockies barely made a blip on the NHL screen in the late 1970s and early '80s, but the Avalanche has been a massive success story since arriving from Quebec City in 1995.

10. SAN JOSE

Sharks fans have never witnessed a Stanley Cup final game. Yet you would be hard-pressed to find a more dedicated following for such a teasing team. It seems only a matter of time before the hockey gods give San Jose fans their just due.

E very hockey fan thinks their city is No. 1, from Nashville to Ottawa and Dallas to Vancouver. The reality is, however, certain cities rank above others due to the local atmosphere, a long association with the NHL, or the team's unmitigated success. Simply put, some places are just more of a hockey town than others.

Montreal is not only one of the league's oldest franchises, it also boasts the most Stanley Cup championships (23) since the NHL formed as well as the most passionate fans around. The sport is covered extensively in both French and English and the team's fortunes are one of the hottest topics in town every day of the week, 52 weeks a year.

Most Successful ● ● ●
Major Junior Franchises

1. TORONTO MARLBOROS (OHA)
Their seven Memorial Cups are the most all-time.

2. MONTREAL JUNIOR CANADIENS (QMJHL/OHA)
Once boasted a team that included Gil Perreault, Richard Martin, Rejean Houle and Marc Tardif.

3. OSHAWA GENERALS (OHL)
Imagine being able to boast that Bobby Orr, Eric Lindros and John Tavares all played for your favorite junior team.

4. PETERBOROUGH PETES (OHL)
Only one Memorial Cup title, but the Petes have graduated more players into the NHL than any other franchise in the world.

5. KAMLOOPS BLAZERS (WHL)
Won three Memorial Cups in a four-year period in the early '90s.

6. KITCHENER RANGERS (OHL)
Two-time national champions, the Rangers have been a highly regarded franchise since 1960.

7. NEW WESTMINSTER BRUINS (WHL)
Ernie 'Punch' McLean's Big, Bad Bruins once ruled the WHL, winning back-to-back Memorial Cups in the late '70s.

8. TORONTO ST. MICHAEL'S MAJORS (OHL)
Franchise enjoyed success at various levels, including four Memorial Cups and as the major provider of talent for the Toronto Maple Leafs.

9. OTTAWA 67'S (OHL)
Brian Kilrea and Co. have proven that junior hockey can operate successfully in an NHL city.

10. PORTLAND WINTER HAWKS (WHL)
Two-time Memorial Cup champion has played a major role in putting the Canadian Hockey League on the map in the United States.

Go to a game between two last-place NHL teams and you aren't likely to have a memorable evening.

But a game between two bottom-of-the-barrel junior teams still has significant meaning. How is that?

Simple: The junior game features 40 players putting it all on the line as they try to make it to the NHL. There is no coasting, no taking a shift off when you are trying to make it to the big leagues.

Junior hockey is the lifeblood of hockey in Canada and the northern United States. It is a reasonably priced alternative for hockey fanatics who relish the opportunity to see some of the game's best players on their way up.

Bobby Orr was already a phenom at age 14 when he played for the Oshawa Generals. Wayne Gretzky played three games with the Peterborough Petes as a 15-year-old call-up (he had three assists in those games) before being drafted by the Sault Ste. Marie Greyhounds. Ray Ferarro scored 108 goals for the WHL's Brandon Wheat Kings in 1983-84, which should have been enough to be named Canadian major junior's player of the year – except that Mario Lemieux scored 133 goals for Laval (QMJHL) in the very same season. The Peterborough Petes have won just one Memorial Cup (1979), but have sent more players to the NHL than any other junior franchise. Scotty Bowman, Roger Neilson and Mike Keenan, among others, started out as coaches there, too.

Junior hockey makes stars out of young men, some of whom go on to professional glory and some of whom fade into oblivion. Over the years, major junior has become big business; it is not unusual, for example, for the London Knights to draw 10,000 fans to a game.

But money aside, there is still something very romantic about the notion of following the fortunes of your local junior team. After all, what else would you do on a Sudbury Saturday Night?

Craziest Fans ● ● ●

1. PHILADELPHIA FLYERS
The town that boos Santa Claus also loves its hockey.

2. NEW YORK RANGERS
Take it from the Blueseaters...seriously, you have no choice.

3. MONTREAL CANADIENS
When Habs fans get too excited, they burn things.

4. TORONTO MAPLE LEAFS
Leaf Nation spans the globe, no matter the on-ice product.

5. CALGARY FLAMES
The Red Mile was an instant scene of adult entertainment during 2004 playoffs.

6. EDMONTON OILERS
Whyte Avenue became Red Mile with stabbings.

7. LOS ANGELES KINGS
Fans invade Anaheim for an annual 'Duck Roast.'

8. NEW YORK ISLANDERS
Hey, someone has to fight the Rangers fans.

9. BUFFALO SABRES
When people own Patrick Kaleta jerseys, you know it's serious.

10. DETROIT RED WINGS
Motown knows how to party, eight legs a week.

Part of the attraction of hockey is the intimacy and interactivity of arenas. Sure, you can get a floor seat at a basketball game, but in hockey you can pound on the glass while your favorite hooligans duke it out. The towns that know this are the ones that give their teams that extra fire, an experience known most frequently throughout the years in Philadelphia and New York. Philadelphia's 'Orange Crush' is always in full throat and on the lookout for anyone in a Devils jersey who dares enter Flyers turf. Ironically, that goes the same for the 'Blue-seaters' at Madison Square Garden, but you can add Isles jerseys on top of the outlawed New Jersey gear.

Fans in Toronto and Buffalo will pack the house no matter how their team is faring in the standings and you don't want to be driving down the main drag in Alberta's two biggest cities if the Flames or Oilers are deep in the playoffs.

And if you're in Detroit, of course, make sure you keep your head up for any flying octopi which may whiz by on their way to the ice.

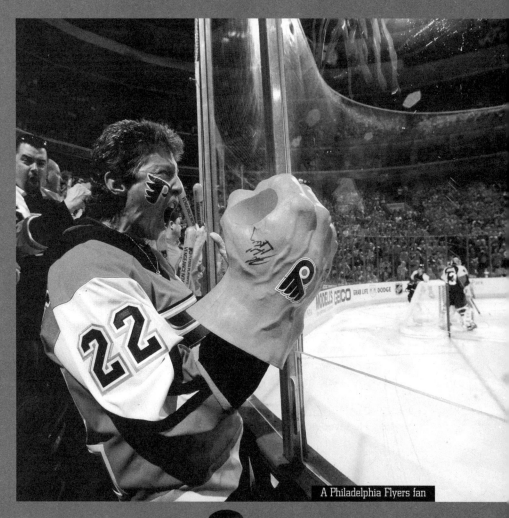

A Philadelphia Flyers fan

Best Owners ● ● ● ●

1. MIKE ILITCH
The Detroit pizza baron took over the Red Wings in the 1980s when they were the NHL's laughingstock and turned them into one of the most successful – and most lucrative – franchises in the league.

2. JOE CATTARINICH
The Canadiens goalie was a player-owner almost 100 years before Mario Lemieux and was instrumental in Montreal signing Georges Vezina.

3. JOHN McMULLEN
He ushered the New Jersey Devils through their moribund years and patiently built the team into a perennial Stanley Cup threat.

4. HARTLAND MOLSON
The Canadian brewing giant took over the Canadiens in 1957 and enhanced the tradition of excellence with a string of Stanley Cups and good hockey people.

5. EDMONTON INVESTORS GROUP
The 34-man conglomerate headed by Cal Nichols kept the Oilers afloat during some very lean years; they were rewarded when they sold to billionaire Darryl Katz in 2008.

6. HARLEY HOTCHKISS
The World War II veteran headed a group that purchased the Atlanta Flames in 1980 and moved the team to Calgary, where it won the Cup in 1989.

7. GEORGE GILLET
The American businessman bought the Canadiens and the Bell Centre for $250 million when nobody wanted them and has watched his investment skyrocket.

8. MARIO LEMIEUX
He saved hockey in Pittsburgh several times as a player, owner and player-owner.

9. CONN SMYTHE

He ran every aspect of the Toronto Maple Leafs from their inception and proved to be a brilliant businessman and hockey operator.

10. ED SNIDER

The former vice-president of the Philadelphia Eagles brought NHL hockey to the city in 1967 and the Flyers have been a model franchise ever since.

Ed Snider

When Mike Ilitch purchased the Detroit Red Wings in 1982, he referred to the franchise as "a sleeping giant waiting for someone to do something with it."

It was sleeping all right. After suffering years of neglect under the Norris family, the Wings had taken almost permanent residence in the lowest part of the NHL standings and fans were ambivalent toward the team. When Ilitch took over, the club had 2,100 season-ticket holders and one of Ilitch's first promotions was to give a car away every game in order to get people to come.

His $9-million investment in the Red Wings paid off, in large part because Ilitch hired the right people immediately and set about to allowing them to do their jobs without the worry of being fired. Even though Ilitch was aggressive and impatient as a businessman, it was his sense of realism and his willingness to be faithful to a natural building process that has made the Red Wings the most successful team in the NHL for the past two decades.

"You're judging a team that has been very good for the past 15 years...very, very good," said Red Wings senior vice-president Jim Devellano. "But the truth of the matter is the 11 years before that, we really had a tough time getting good. It's easy now to look at things and say they're great and they are, but it wasn't easy. It wasn't a quick transformation...no chance was it a quick transformation."

The first thing Ilitch did when he purchased the Red Wings was to install Devellano as GM and it turned out to be a stroke of genius. One of the first players Devellano signed for the Wings' minor league team was a 5-foot-8 goaltender named Ken Holland, not knowing that a quarter-century later, Holland would develop into one of the top GMs in the NHL.

Ilitch wasn't always patient, however. In 1985, things seemed to be moving a little too slowly, so Ilitch ordered Devellano to go out and sign the nine best college free agents in the country. The Wings overhauled their roster that summer with a ton of free agents, the most prominent of whom was Ray Staszak, a college star pegged for great things in the NHL.

"After doing all that, we finished dead-last that year with 40 points," Devellano said. "But Mike never blamed anybody for it. It was something he wanted to try and do and his commitment was there and his passion was there."

As a young man in Detroit, Ilitch was a promising shortstop who dreamed of a career in the major leagues. We're left to wonder what would have happened had Ilitch's baseball career not been derailed by a knee injury.

"He stuck to it and we stuck to it," Devellano said, "and eventually, the pieces fell into place."

Mike Ilitch

Wackiest Teams ● ● ●

1. CALIFORNIA GOLDEN SEALS/OAKLAND SEALS
White skates, red ink.

2. NEW YORK ISLANDERS (1990s)
Mad Mike and the owner who never was.

3. OTTAWA SENATORS (1990s)
If anyone knows how to run a draft, call Mel Bridgeman.

4. WASHINGTON CAPITALS (1970s)
Taking awful hockey to new lows.

5. HARTFORD WHALERS (1982-83)
Hockey players wear socks. The long-pantsed Whalers showed why.

6. ST. LOUIS BLUES (1980s)
Became a dog's breakfast under Ralston-Purina.

7. TORONTO MAPLE LEAFS (1980s)
Harold. Ballard.

8. NEW YORK RANGERS (1950S-60s)
Getting sent to Broadway was a punishment back then.

9. MIGHTY DUCKS OF ANAHEIM (1990s)
Disney's magic did not extend to hockey.

10. NEW YORK ISLANDERS (PRESENT)
Where goalies carry briefcases.

As a frontier sport, hockey has had more than its fair share of characters. Sometimes, however, those characters can drive an entire franchise to lunacy. From crazy owners to sad-sack rosters, the NHL has housed many wacky teams over the years.

Some have been just plain bad (Washington in the 1970s and the Rangers in the '50s and '60s), while others upped the ante by looking dreadful (Hartford's infamous Cooperall pants).

But the team that takes the cake is the California Seals. They became the Oakland Seals, then the California Golden Seals, then the Cleveland Barons, who were then absorbed by the Minnesota North Stars. As one of the original NHL expansion teams, the Seals were best known for a laughable experiment in which the team wore white skates instead of the traditional black. Coupled with the team's gold and green uniforms, it was quite a sight when the Seals took to the ice – and it usually didn't end in a win.

Another team which stumbled out the gate (but managed to recover) was the second incarnation of the Ottawa Senators. At the expansion draft in 1992, GM Mel Bridgeman famously lost his list of eligible players and the Senators were twice forced to reselect when they attempted to pick an unclaimable player. On the ice, the Sens were dreadful in the early days and the high draft pick which came with one of those basement performances, Alexandre Daigle, would turn out to be one of the biggest busts in NHL history.

But if you're talking about "Mickey Mouse" franchises, look no further than the team owned by Disney. The Mighty Ducks of Anaheim (who would finally become respectable under new ownership and a change to a normal name, the Anaheim

Alexei
Yashin

Ducks) were of course named after a children's movie. The Mighty Ducks also featured some of the worst sweaters in league history; the team's standard purple and aquamarine fare, plus the infamously bad third jersey featuring mascot Wild Wing crashing skywards through ice.

Ownership often can turn a team into a joke. The Toronto Maple Leafs under Harold Ballard in the 1980s are the gold standard. The team was always lousy and Ballard was consistently offensive towards many people. In one of his less venomous tirades, he suggested coach Roger Neilson step behind the bench with a paper bag over his head. (Neilson declined.)

The St. Louis Blues also went through a rough patch in the early '80s with ownership playing the villain. To say the Blues were treated like dog food by Ralston-Purina is only too apt. After purchasing the financially struggling franchise in 1977, the corporation had a brief love affair with the team before losing interest by 1983. When a sale to Saskatoon was blocked, the company essentially abandoned the team, who in turn missed the '83 draft.

While the Blues recovered, the Islanders have had all sorts of wacky seasons. In the 1990s, the venerable franchise was nearly bought by John Spano, who would later be convicted of bank fraud in connection with the attempted purchase. In the meantime, GM 'Mad' Mike Milbury was trading away future franchise players such as Zdeno Chara, Roberto Luongo, Jason Spezza and Olli Jokinen (not to mention passing on Dany Heatley and Marian Gaborik in the draft) for Oleg Kvasha and Mark Parrish, infamous millstone Alexei Yashin and the right to draft Rick DiPietro. As if that wasn't enough, the Isles swapped their traditional jerseys for a fisherman logo that was universally derided due to its similarity to various frozen seafood company mascots. It goes without saying that Rangers fans still taunt their crosstown rivals with chants of "Fish sticks! Fish sticks!"

To complete the circle, the Isles are now run by computer titan Charles Wang, who signed DiPietro to a 15-year contract, fired GM Neil Smith after 40 days on the job and replaced him with then-backup goalie Garth Snow. But at least they're wearing proper uniforms again.

The winning goal for Belarus shot by **Vladimir Kopat** (not shown) trickles in after it bounced off Sweden's goalie **Tommy Salo**.

Jaw-Dropping
Moments

1. MIRACLE ON ICE
Team USA shocks Soviet Union and beats Finland for 1980 Olympic gold medal.

2. PATRIK STEFAN'S DISASTROUS EMPTY-NET MISCUE IN 2007
How did he miss? And how did he feel when Edmonton went
the other way and tied it up?

3. 'THE GOAL' BY ALEX OVECHKIN IN 2005-06
Spinning, falling, twisting, turning...there'll never be another goal like it.

4. BELARUS BEATS SWEDEN WITH A SHOT OFF TOMMY SALO'S HELMET AT 2002 OLYMPICS
Swedish newspapers the next day had photos of every player
on the team under the headline: "Traitors!"

5. MIRACLE ON MANCHESTER, 1982
It's not often a team rallies from a 5-0 third period deficit in the playoffs.

6. MIKE LEGG'S LACROSSE-STYLE GOAL AGAINST UNIVERSITY OF MINNESOTA IN 1996
Look for an updated version coming soon to a shootout near you.

7. RON HEXTALL BECOMES FIRST NHL GOALIE TO SHOOT PUCK INTO EMPTY NET FOR A GOAL IN 1987
And for good measure, he scored in the playoffs in 1989.

8. MAREK MALIK'S SHOOTOUT GOAL IN 2005
Nothing like watching a 6-foot-6 stay-at-home defenseman successfully attempt
the stick-between-the-legs deke. As the 30th shooter in the shootout, no less.

9. SCOTT STEVENS FLATTENS ERIC LINDROS IN THE 2000 PLAYOFFS
Now we know what happens when an immovable object
meets an unstoppable force.

10. RUSSIANS STUN CANADA 7-3 IN GAME 1 OF 1972 SUMMIT SERIES
Hmm, maybe this won't be an easy eight-game sweep like everybody says...

They are the moments burned into the consciousness of every hockey fan. If you were watching it happen in real time, you were likely overcome by confusion at first: "Did I just see what I think I saw?" Then, depending on which team you were cheering for, your stomach filled with either butterflies or sickness. In the end, either elation or dejection.

No Canadian hockey fan thought the 1972 Summit Series was going to be close, let alone one in which the Soviet Union would be leading Game 1 4-3 with 10 minutes to play. The jaw-dropper came when the Soviets scored three more times on the Canucks for a decisive 7-3 victory, shocking an overconfident nation watching at home.

In 1980, it was the Soviets' turn to be shocked, when a plucky bunch of American college kids found themselves tied with the Big Red Machine at the Lake Placid Olympics. Mike Eruzione then famously potted the go-ahead goal and Team USA was on its way to clinching gold.

In a more recent Olympic shocker, gold medal favorites Sweden were tied with lowly Belarus when Vladimir Kopat fired a long slapshot from the red line that bounced off Swedish goalie Tommy Salo's helmet, then dribbled into the net, securing a Belarus victory and bouncing Sweden from the medal round.

In the NHL, the Edmonton Oilers found a similar playoff fate when the Los Angeles Kings turned a 5-0 third period deficit into a 6-5 overtime win and eventually a series upset in what came to be known as the 'Miracle on Manchester.'

But some moments are jaw-dropping because they displayed something previously thought to be impossible, or at least unthought of at the time.

When the University of Michigan's Mike Legg picked the puck up on the blade of his stick lacrosse-style and then proceeded to flip it into the top corner of the Minnesota net, it was the first time the trick had been used in a big-game situation. As well, Marek Malik's between-the-legs shootout goal – which occurred just a few weeks into the 2005-06 season, the NHL's first campaign with the new tie-breaking format – would become the gold standard in that area of skill.

When unforgettable moments are mentioned, a recent name that pops up is Alex Ovechkin and his sliding-on-his-back goal against Phoenix in 2006. Known simply as 'The Goal,' repeated viewings do not diminish its greatness.

But for true incomprehensibility, nothing will ever beat the set of circumstances which essentially ended the career of Patrik Stefan, the No. 1 overall draft pick in 1999. Already considered a washout in Atlanta, Stefan was playing in Dallas when he parlayed an Edmonton turnover into a breakaway towards an empty net with a one-goal lead and 10 seconds to play. As Stefan attempted to gently guide the puck into the net, the biscuit hit a rut in the ice and bounced over his stick, causing Stefan to fall and sweep the puck backwards. The disc was recovered by the Oilers, who quickly moved it up the ice, where Ales Hemsky would ultimately bury the shocking game-tying goal with two seconds remaining. The Stars would win in extra time, but Stefan never recovered. He would play briefly in Switzerland before retiring at age 26 due to nagging injuries.

Team USA celebrates its 4-3 victory over the Soviet Union in the 1980 Olympic semifinal.

Biggest
Busts

1. RAY MARTYNIUK (5th overall, MONTREAL, 1970)
"Can't miss kid" didn't play an NHL game.

2. ALEXANDRE VOLCHKOV (3rd overall, Washington, 1996)
Russian sniper was too lazy for professional game.

3. DANIEL DORE (5th overall, Quebec, 1988)
Power forward never hit his potential (or anything else).

4. ALEXANDRE DAIGLE (1st overall, Ottawa, 1993)
Scored 51 points as 21-year-old, but hit 30-point mark only once more.

5. SCOTT SCISSONS (6th overall, NY Islanders, 1990)
Played in two NHL games and spent most of his time in the IHL.

6. JASON BONSIGNORE (4th overall, Edmonton, 1994)
Scored 22 goals in the OHL at age 16, but never played full NHL season.

7. DAVE CHYZOWSKI (2nd overall, NY Islanders, 1989)
THN's 1989 Draft Preview had it right, calling Chyzowski
a "boom or bust" prospect.

8. PATRIK STEFAN (1st overall, Atlanta, 1999)
Czech star and No. 1 selection never scored 15 goals in a season.

9. DANIEL TKACZUK (6th overall, Calgary, 1997)
The next Ron Francis played 19 NHL games as a 21-year-old
and never made it back.

10. ALEXANDER SVITOV (3rd overall, Tampa Bay, 2001)
Youngest player to skate in the Russian Elite League
topped out at 18 points in the NHL.

In determining the biggest busts in history, let's agree there is a different set of expectations for first overall picks compared to later selections. Alexandre Daigle (especially) and Patrik Stefan were very highly hyped and expected to produce at all-star levels in the NHL. While neither came anywhere close to fulfilling those lofty expectations, both still played more than 400 NHL games. Yes, they still busted – and how – but let's give them some credit for making it to the big leagues and sticking around for a little while.

On the other hand, there's Ray Martyniuk, who won just about everything a goalie could in the WCHL in the late 1960s. Labeled the "can't miss kid," Martyniuk didn't play a second in the NHL. Surely, that makes him a bigger bust than Daigle or Stefan. We think it does; in fact, we think it makes him the biggest bust in NHL history.

Another gauge on how big of a bust a player was is to look at how long it took them to end their hockey careers altogether. Daniel Dore was expected to be a forceful power forward for his hometown Quebec Nordiques, but was never able to cope with the pressure of playing in

Alexandre
Daigle

his backyard. Not only did Dore play just 17 NHL games, his hockey career was over six years after he was drafted. In 1994 he started playing for Montreal…in a roller hockey league.

Alexandre Volchkov and Scott Scissons also fall into the category of fast flameouts. Volchkov, a star with the OHL's Barrie Colts in the mid-'90s, soon earned a reputation as a floater and made his way into an NHL lineup for only three games. He returned to Russia in 2000. Scissons, a 40-goal man in the WHL, was selected by the Islanders one pick after Pittsburgh took Jaromir Jagr in 1990, but had nowhere near the Czech star's impact. He played in only two NHL games, spending most of his pro career in the IHL before disappearing from the game a mere five years after he was drafted.

You'd think the Islanders would learn. The year before picking Scissons, they had drafted another WHL sniper, Dave Chyzowski, with the second overall choice (Mats Sundin went No. 1 to Quebec). After being rushed to the NHL – he played 90 games for New York before he turned 20 – Chyzowski ended up with 15 goals in 126 career games. After several seasons in the IHL, he spent seven years in Europe – far, far away from the NHL.

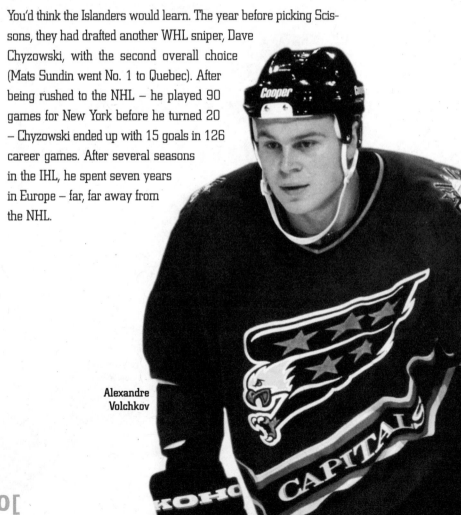

Alexandre
Volchkov

Most Significant ● ● ● ●
Contracts

1. BOBBY HULL
Five-year deal with Winnipeg Jets of WHA paid $1 million.

2. ALEXANDRE DAIGLE
Five-year, $12.5-million rookie deal a big part of 1994 lockout.

3. ULF STERNER
First European-trained player to sign an NHL contract in 1965.

4. SERGEI PRIAKIN
The Flames signed the first Soviet-trained skater in 1988.

5. RICK DIPIETRO
15-year contract the first long-term commitment in salary cap era; Alex Ovechkin, Mike Richards follow.

6. SCOTT STEVENS
Agreed to offer sheet from St. Louis in 1990, starting a trend of compensation.

7. ALEX OVECHKIN
Became NHL's first $100-million man with 13-year, $124-million contract.

8. WAYNE GRETZKY
21-year personal services deal with Peter Pocklington kept Gretzky out of the WHA dispersal draft.

9. MANON RHEAUME
First woman to sign NHL contract.

10. RENFREW MILLIONAIRES
NHA team bought all-star lineup in first season of 1909-10, including Cyclone Taylor.

The NHL, like any business, pays its employees to perform, and perform well. Just like any other business, NHL teams work in a free market and have to pay for it. So while player contracts have been common throughout NHL history, every once in a while one grabs headlines and changes how the system functions.

When the WHA's Winnipeg Jets signed Bobby Hull away from the Chicago Black Hawks in 1972, it not only kick-started the rival league with one of the game's biggest stars, it also ushered in a new era of expense. To sweeten the pot and help persuade The Golden Jet to leave the NHL, the five-year deal fronted a $1-million signing bonus, making Hull hockey's first million-dollar player. Not only did this contract lead to a rise in all player salaries, it also led other NHL stars – such as Gerry Cheevers, J.C. Tremblay and Derek Sanderson – to sign on with the WHA.

The exercise of offering wads of cash to lure in stars began in the National Hockey Association – the NHL's most important precursor and closest cousin – when the Renfrew (Ont.) Millionaires signed Cyclone Taylor ($5,000) and Lester ($3,000) and Frank Patrick ($2,000) for the 1909-10 season, which ultimately caused their bankruptcy after two years.

From Hull, the new money game took 20 years to escalate into a matter of contention between employer and employee. When the Ottawa Senators signed Alexandre Daigle to a $12.5-million deal after drafting him first overall in 1993 – before he even stepped on an NHL ice surface – owners were at their tipping point and forced a lockout in 1994.

Bobby Hull

In the salary cap era beginning in 2005, the point of debate has shifted from contract amount to contract length. Rick DiPietro's 15-year pact with the New York Islanders in 2006 left many scratching their heads and pointing fingers at inexperienced owner Charles Wang, but decade-plus deals to stars Alex Ovechkin (13 years) and Mike Richards (12 years) soon followed.

Best ●●●●●●●
Wrist Shots

1. JOE SAKIC
2. DENNIS HULL
3. MARK HOWE
4. RAY BOURQUE
5. WENDEL CLARK
6. VACLAV NEDOMANSKY
7. CHARLIE CONACHER
8. REGGIE LEACH
9. BABE DYE
10. RICK MACLEISH

No hockey player gets the word 'rifle' in their nickname without boasting a heck of a shot.

Another indicator you can let the puck go? Scoring a league-record 19 goals in one playoff season.

Reggie Leach earned the moniker 'The Riverton Rifle' based on the heavy wrist shot he used to beat goalies during the 1970s. After racking up 61 goals with the Flyers during the 1975-76 regular season, Leach added 19 more in 16 playoff games to establish a record that was equaled by Edmonton's Jari Kurri in 1985. Leach was awarded the Conn Smythe Trophy that year despite the fact Philadelphia lost the Stanley Cup to Montreal.

Just as the Flyers liked to intimidate opponents with physical play, Leach tried to strike fear in goalies' hearts with his rocket. One of the stoppers he had success against was the Canadiens' Ken Dryden, something Leach attributes, at least partially, to intimidation.

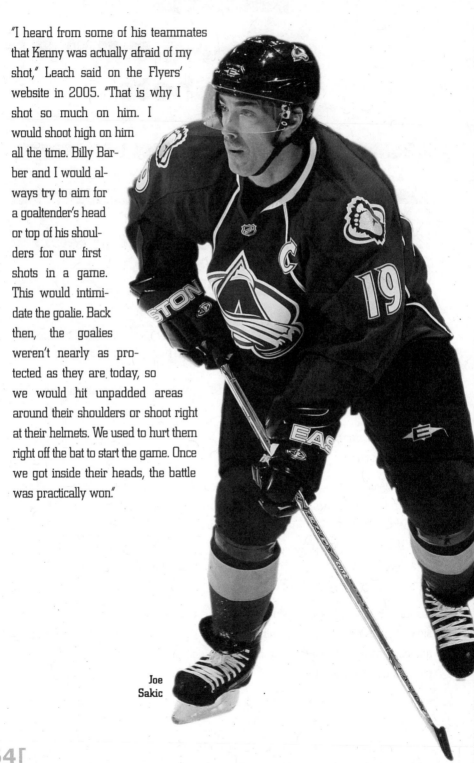

"I heard from some of his teammates that Kenny was actually afraid of my shot," Leach said on the Flyers' website in 2005. "That is why I shot so much on him. I would shoot high on him all the time. Billy Barber and I would always try to aim for a goaltender's head or top of his shoulders for our first shots in a game. This would intimidate the goalie. Back then, the goalies weren't nearly as protected as they are today, so we would hit unpadded areas around their shoulders or shoot right at their helmets. We used to hurt them right off the bat to start the game. Once we got inside their heads, the battle was practically won."

Joe
Sakic

Most Successful ● ● ●
NCAA Programs

1. MICHIGAN
9 NCAA titles, 22 Frozen Four appearances

2. NORTH DAKOTA
7 NCAA titles, 16 Frozen Four appearances

3. DENVER
7 NCAA titles, 13 Frozen Four appearances

4. BOSTON UNIVERSITY
4 NCAA titles, 20 Frozen Four appearances

5. BOSTON COLLEGE
3 NCAA titles, 21 Frozen Four appearances

6. MINNESOTA
5 NCAA titles, 19 Frozen Four appearances

7. WISCONSIN
6 NCAA titles, 11 Frozen Four appearances

8. MICHIGAN STATE
3 NCAA titles, 11 Frozen Four appearances

9. HARVARD
1 NCAA title, 12 Frozen Four appearances

10. COLORADO COLLEGE
2 NCAA titles, 10 Frozen Four appearances

The Maize and Blue of Michigan have been a force in U.S. college hockey right from the start, winning six of the first 10 NCAA titles and finishing no worse than third in that opening decade under coach Vic Heyliger. More recently, the Wolverines have made the NCAA tournament every year since 1991 and took home the championship in '96 and '98. In terms of talent, alumni include established NHLers such as Marty Turco, Brendan Morrison and Mike Komisarek, as well as rising stars Andrew Cogliano and Jack Johnson. The legendary Red Berenson has coached the Wolverines since 1984.

Loathed on the ice by Midwest rivals Minnesota and Wisconsin and controversial off of it because of a steadfast refusal to change its Fighting Sioux logo and moniker, North Dakota is nevertheless another perennial challenger for conference and national crowns, with alumni including Ed Belfour and Jonathan Toews.

Also in the WCHA, Denver has been a frequent guest at the Frozen Four and currently wreaks havoc under coach George Gwozdecky, who has two national titles and three conference crowns to his credit. Alumni include Paul Stastny, Keith Magnuson and Bill Masterton.

Out on the East Coast, there is one college rivalry that rules them all: Boston University vs. Boston College. The Terriers boast a proud history of success, as well as producing NHLers such

The **Michigan Wolverines** are an NCAA powerhouse.

as Tony Amonte, Adrian Aucoin and Chris Drury, plus Miracle on Ice hero Mike Eruzione. Boston University has dominated the city's famous Beanpot tournament, winning 28 times, twice the amount of runner-up Boston College and as many as Harvard, Boston College and Northeastern combined.

Of course, if you're looking for the most recent bragging rights in Beantown, they belong to Boston College's Eagles. They're the reigning NCAA champs and the Hockey East powerhouse has produced some of America's best players, including Brian Leetch and Joe Mullen, as well as current NHL stars Brian Gionta and Bill Guerin.

Back in the Midwest, you'll find another tandem of rival foes, Minnesota and Wisconsin. Vying for the same geographic talent pool has made for a lot of feistiness in the heartland, but from the Broten brothers to Erik Johnson and Thomas Vanek of Golden Gophers fame to Wisconsin alumni such as Gary Suter, Brian Rafalski and Dany Heatley, the teams have clearly learned to share — sometimes.

The **Wolverines** have celebrated often in their illustrious history.

Best Goal ●●●●
Celebrations

1. BOBBY ORR'S CUP-CLINCHER

Perhaps the most enduring image in hockey history is Orr's game-winning, Stanley Cup-clinching goal against St. Louis in 1970. The photo that ran in the Boston Globe showed the game's greatest defenseman with his arms raised and his body nearly parallel to the ice, giving him a distinct Superman-style appearance. The way Orr played, it was a perfect fit – and one that still carries much luster to this day.

2. DAVE 'TIGER' WILLIAMS

While he was most famous for his pugilistic skills, Williams' act after a goal – where he put his stick between his legs and rode it down the ice like some sort of makeshift motorcycle – also added greatly to his legend.

3. ALEX OVECHKIN

The Russian superstar's passion for the game is apparent after every one of his many goals; often, he'll leap and bounce off of the rink glass as his 10,000-watt smile lights up the entire arena. Nobody displays the joy of the game better.

4. PAUL HENDERSON'S SUMMIT SERIES WINNER

Like the image of Orr's famous Cup-winning goal, Henderson's series-winning marker for Team Canada in 1972 will live on forever in the hearts of Canadians and hockey fans everywhere. There is nothing particularly different about it – Henderson is standing with his arms raised as teammate Yvan Cournoyer emphatically embraces him – but nobody will ever forget that magical moment and improbable comeback against the then-unknown Soviet Union team.

5. THEOREN FLEURY AND 'THE LONG SLIDE'

While a member of the Calgary Flames, Fleury scored in overtime of the 1991 Smythe Division semifinal against Edmonton to force a Game 7. He was so elated, he skated from one corner of the arena, past his teammates at the blueline, and slid/rolled skates-first past center ice and into the boards at the other end of the rink before his teammates piled onto him.

6. TEEMU SELANNE AND 'THE SKEET SHOT'

He only did it once (when he broke Mike Bossy's record for goals by a rookie), but when Selanne was playing for the Winnipeg Jets and potted his 54th goal of the 1992-93 campaign against the Quebec Nordiques, he tossed his right glove into the air and pretended to shoot at it with his stick.

7. MIKE FOLIGNO

The former Red Wings and Sabres gritty great was renowned for finishing off just about every one of his 355 career NHL goals with a two-footed leap into the air. White men can jump; it just doesn't look pretty.

8. MILAN HEJDUK AND 'THE DIVE AND SWIM'

Hejduk's overtime goal against Dallas in 2000 caused the Avs winger to skate toward center ice, dive into the air, and mimic a few swimming strokes before he slid to a halt.

9. MIRO SATAN AND 'THE PHONE CALL'

In 2004, Buffalo Sabres winger Satan was believed to be on the trade block and was told to "expect a phone call." So when he scored in Toronto just days before the trade deadline, he celebrated by taking off his glove and miming a phone conversation. The Sabres never did deal him, though.

10. MAREK MALIK'S REGAL SHOOTOUT GOAL

The New York Rangers defenseman wowed fans with a between-the-legs goal that ended a marathon shootout session against Washington in November of 2005. Even better was his reaction afterwards, where he merely held up his left hand to acknowledge the wild cheering at Madison Square Garden. The Queen of England would've been proud.

Alex Ovechkin

Teemu Selanne

For the most part, the cele-bration of a hockey goal is as understated and humble as the players themselves. The game's conservative nature dic-tates that players who score treat their success with a degree of stoicism normally seen only in judges and priests, so it's far more likely you'll see them uti-lizing poker faces than beaming smiles and flailing arms.

But the reserved nature of most players is what helps make hockey's most memorable goal celebrations stick in the minds of the sport's fans. And, whether it's a one-time, spontaneous out-burst, or, in rarer cases, a sig-nature move, the game does have a number of celebrations worth noting (and ranking).

Best Lines ● ● ● ● ●

1. THE TRIPLE CROWN LINE
Marcel Dionne, Charlie Simmer,
Dave Taylor (Los Angeles Kings)

2. THE PRODUCTION LINE
Gordie Howe, Sid Abel, Ted Lindsay (Detroit Red Wings)

3. THE PUNCH LINE
Maurice Richard, Elmer Lach, Hector 'Toe' Blake
(Montreal Canadiens)

4. THE LILCO LINE
Mike Bossy, Bryan Trottier, Clark Gillies
(New York Islanders)

5. THE FRENCH CONNECTION
Rene Robert, Gilbert Perreault, Richard Martin
(Buffalo Sabres)

6. THE G-A-G LINE
Vic Hadfield, Jean Ratelle, Rod Gilbert
(New York Rangers)

7. THE ESPO LINE
Wayne Cashman, Phil Esposito, Ken Hodge
(Boston Bruins)

8. THE KID LINE
Harvey 'Busher' Jackson, Joe Primeau, Charlie Conacher
(Toronto Maple Leafs)

9. THE DYNASTY LINE
Guy Lafleur, Jacques Lemaire, Steve Shutt or Pete Mahovlich
(Montreal Canadiens)

10. THE LEGION OF DOOM
Mikael Renberg, Eric Lindros, John LeClair
(Philadelphia Flyers)

THE FRENCH CONNECTION

MARTIN PERREAULT ROBERT
THE FRENCH CONNECTION

RENE ROBERT 14 1972-1979

GILBERT PERREAULT 11 1970-1986

RICHARD MARTIN 7 1971-198

A view of the banners of Rene Robert, Gilbert Perreault and Richard Martin that hang at HSBC Arena in Buffalo.

The Triple Crown Line made some sweet music on the ice. The magic, however, didn't translate to the studio.

Not content to merely embarrass opposing goalies, Marcel Dionne, Charlie Simmer and Dave Taylor put their dignity aside in 1979 and had a little fun while recording the single *Please Forgive My Misconduct Last Night*. The track was released under the name 'Marcel Dionne and the Puck-Tones' and the proceeds – which surely paled in comparison to the trio's point totals – went to diabetes research.

The other side of the 45 featured Phil Esposito and a number of other Rangers performing a little number called *Hockey Sock Rock*. It's fair to say Dionne and Espo, Nos. 4 and 5 on the NHL's all-time goal-scoring list, were better at their day jobs.

Longevity and equal share of the workload were two heavily weighted factors in establishing the NHL's best lines of all-time. So while Wayne Gretzky and Jari Kurri were a dominant duo, it's difficult to lump the entire line with the best ever considering tough guy Dave Semenko was usually riding shotgun. (Uh, no offense, Mr. Semenko, sir.)

Before he was making records with the Rangers, Esposito and his Bruins linemates tore up the NHL during the 1970-71 season. The big center led the league with 76 goals and 152 points and was flanked by the NHL's No. 4 point-getter, Ken Hodge, and the No. 7 scorer, Wayne Cashman.

Some lines were more fluid than others. While Guy Lafleur and Steve Shutt usually played together on Montreal's dynasty teams of the late '70s, both Jacques Lemaire and Pete Mahovlich skated with the pair at different times. Like Shutt and Lafleur, Mahovlich was a natural winger, prompting the quick-witted Shutt to rename that troika The Donut Line because it had no center.

The G-A-G Line's name was a little malleable, too, depending on how things were going. Vic Hadfield, Jean Ratelle and Rod Gilbert earned their original nickname with the Rangers because they were good for a "Goal A Game." But when production picked up, they'd sometimes be referred to as the T-A-G Line – "Two goals A Game."

Mike Bossy, Bryan Trottier and Clark Gillies ignited a lot of red lights for the Islanders during nearly a decade together, which prompted their line's LILCO moniker (Long Island Lighting Company).

Greatest ● ● ● ●
Draft Classes

1. 1979 – Mark Messier, Ray Bourque, Mike Gartner, Michel Goulet, Kevin Lowe, Glenn Anderson, Mats Naslund, Rick Vaive

It's the draft by which all others are measured.

2. 1984 – Mario Lemieux, Patrick Roy, Brett Hull, Luc Robitaille, Gary Roberts, Kirk Muller, Stephane Richer

Two of the best players ever in Lemieux and Roy, two of the best snipers ever in Hull and Robitaille.

3. 1988 – Mike Modano, Teemu Selanne, Alex Mogilny, Jeremy Roenick, Rod Brind'Amour, Mark Recchi

Trevor Linden and Tony Amonte also selected in Year Of The Forward.

4. 1981 – Dale Hawerchuk, Chris Chelios, Ron Francis, Scott Stevens, Doug Gilmour, Dave Andreychuk

Centers of attention and defensemen of destruction.

5. 1990 – Jaromir Jagr, Martin Brodeur, Peter Bondra, Keith Tkachuk, Keith Primeau, Owen Nolan

Perhaps the best forward and goalie of their generation, plus power forwards, too.

6. 1971 – Guy Lafleur, Marcel Dionne, Larry Robinson, Rick Martin, Terry O'Reilly

The Canadiens especially like this draft year.

7. 2003 – Eric Staal, Dion Phaneuf, Thomas Vanek, Marc-Andre Fleury, Ryan Getzlaf

Check back in 10 years; this draft might turn out to be the best ever.

8. 1970 – Gilbert Perreault, Darryl Sittler, Billy Smith, Reggie Leach, Rick MacLeish

Franchise faces and a scary-good goalie.

9. 2005 – Sidney Crosby, Paul Stastny, Anze Kopitar, Carey Price, Marc Staal

The kids are better than alright.

10. 1997 – Joe Thornton, Roberto Luongo, Marian Hossa, Olli Jokinen, Brenden Morrow

This class needs Cups to graduate.

Since the first NHL entry draft in 1969, teams have landed franchise players while others went bust. And some draft classes have been deeper and stronger than others, thanks to the legacy of the Hall of Famers and Stanley Cup champions each year produced.

No matter how obsessive scouting gets, or how many mock drafts are produced and pored over before the big day, it's fair to say the feat achieved by NHL teams at the 1979 draft will never be repeated: Every first round pick that year played at least seven NHL seasons. Not only were the players consistent, but many were stupendous. Rob Ramage, the No. 1 pick by the Colorado Rockies, had a very distinguished career, though not a flashy one. But behind him came Hall of Famers such as Mike Gartner (No. 4), Ray Bourque (No. 8) and Michel Goulet (No. 20). "Buried" in the draft were stars such as Hall of Famers Mark

Mark
Messier

Messier and Glenn Anderson, as well as Guy Carbonneau and Neal Broten. Perhaps one way this class tipped its hand to the scouts is that many of the youngsters had already played a season in the WHA, which helped acclimate them to the pro game much sooner than other classes.

In terms of big-name status, it's impossible to beat the 1984 draft crew. The obvious first choice was Mario Lemieux by Pittsburgh, as The Magnificent One was coming off a 133-goal, 282-point season with Laval in the QMJHL. Attempting to stop Lemieux in some of those games was Granby Bisons goaltender Patrick Roy, who landed in Montreal with the 51st pick and went on to become one of the best stoppers of all-time. And if it seems impossible that a talent such as Roy would be picked so deep, look for Brett Hull later on the board: one of the purest goal-scorers ever went to Calgary with the 117th pick.

With the exception of 1979, every draft class has had its first round blunders, but in terms of depth in a class, 2003 has come closer than any to matching 1979's prowess. Goalie Marc-Andre Fleury led the charge in '03, followed by Eric Staal, Nathan Horton and Nik Zherdev. The first "bust" of the round didn't come until No. 12, when the Rangers whiffed with Hugh Jessiman. Even after that, however, teams were coming out with gems, such as New Jersey's Zach Parise (No. 17) and the Anaheim duo of Ryan Getzlaf (No. 19) and Corey Perry (No. 28).

Best Defensive ● ● ● ●
Defensemen

1. BOBBY ORR
The Bruins legend led the NHL in plus-minus rating a record six times, including an all-time best plus-124 in 1970-71.

2. NICKLAS LIDSTROM
The brilliance of the Red Wings captain is as apparent in his own end as any other part of the ice.

3. DOUG HARVEY
Seven-time Norris winner is No. 6 on THN's list of the top 100 players of all-time.

4. ROD LANGWAY
Capitals blueliner excelled enough at defending to gain Hall of Fame honors in 2002.

5. LARRY ROBINSON
'Big Bird' came close to Orr's record by registering an amazing plus-120 for Montreal in 1976-77.

6. EDDIE SHORE
Rugged Bruins blueliner was named league MVP four times.

7. BILL WHITE
Talk about a late-blooming defenseman – Black Hawk blueliner didn't skate in first NHL game until age 28.

8. SCOTT STEVENS
Few used the physical brand of play to intimidate opponents better than the Devils captain.

9. RAY BOURQUE
Famous for his offensive skills, the longtime Bruin was also a neutralizing force.

10. TIM HORTON
Strong and physical, opposing forwards avoided this Maple Leaf at all costs.

Pretty much every defenseman who played before Bobby Orr arrived was, by definition, a defensive specialist. If you played on the back line back in the 1950s or earlier, your one and only responsibility (unless your name was Red Kelly, Doug Harvey or Eddie Shore) was shutting down the opposition. Don't worry about scoring; that's what forwards are for. But Orr's emergence in the late 1960s changed that way of thinking. Suddenly, defensemen dared to carry the puck over center ice and get actively involved in the offense. Suddenly, every NHL roster included "two-way" and "all-around" defensemen, and "mobility" and "a transition game" became attributes that every blueliner needed.

Larry Robinson

Well, not quite. Playing solid and simple stay-at-home defense never really went out of vogue, it just wasn't noticed as much. Serge Savard and Ken Morrow and Kevin Lowe and Craig Ludwig continued to do what they did best – block shots, play the body and keep the front of the crease clear.

Meanwhile, it's not as though Orr's offensive game precluded him from playing defense; in fact, quite the opposite. His speed and skating combined with his quick stick and physical style made him very effective at relieving opponents of the puck and turning the play the other way. You didn't want to go near Orr's side of the ice; he'd strip the puck off you and skate it out of danger in the wink of an eye. Just because he didn't remain in his own zone all game doesn't mean Orr didn't dominate on defense; it just means he dominated in other zones, too.

Rod Langway didn't have Orr's speed or skating ability – nobody did, but especially not Langway – but he was a prototype hard-rock defender who blocked shots like a wannabe goalie and took care of business behind his own blueline. Langway was big, physical and did the dirty work in the corners that is the hallmark of every "defensive" defenseman.

"I am honored to be recognized by the Hall of Fame for my 'old school' contributions, in the manner of Bill White or Doug Harvey," said Langway after he was granted entry to the Hall of Fame in 2002. "As a defensive specialist, I am particularly gratified for this recognition."

Bobby Orr

Best ●●●●●
Dynamic Duos

Wayne Gretzky and Jari Kurri

1. ONE-TWO PUNCH: WAYNE GRETZKY AND JARI KURRI
Edmonton, 1980-88; Los Angeles, 1991-95

2. COACH & GM: SAM POLLOCK AND SCOTTY BOWMAN
Montreal, 1971-78

3. GOALIE TANDEM: JACQUES PLANTE AND GLENN HALL
St Louis, 1968-70

4. INDIVIDUAL TALENTS: MARIO LEMIEUX AND JAROMIR JAGR
Pittsburgh, 1990-97, 2000-01

5. FORWARD & DEFENSEMAN COMBO: PHIL ESPOSITO AND BOBBY ORR
Boston, 1967-75

6. OFFENSIVE DEFENSEMEN: LARRY ROBINSON AND GUY LAPOINTE
Montreal, 1972-82

7. SHUTDOWN PAIR: SCOTT STEVENS AND KEN DANEYKO
New Jersey, 1991-2003

8. FACEOFF MEN: ROD BRIND'AMOUR AND RON FRANCIS
Carolina, 1999-2004

9. YOUNG GUNS: SIDNEY CROSBY AND EVGENI MALKIN
Pittsburgh, 2006-present

10. FIGHTERS: BOB PROBERT AND JOEY KOCUR
Detroit, 1985-91

Without a doubt, hockey's most decorated dynamic duo is Wayne Gretzky and Jari Kurri. "Gretzky to Kurri…he shoots, he scores!" is a refrain that still rings in the ears of Oilers fans. The pair not only produced more goals than any other tandem before or since, but they also teamed up to lead Edmonton to four Stanley Cups. And a few years after 'The Trade' in 1988, Kurri followed Gretzky to Los Angeles to continue their excellence. While playing on the same team for 13 seasons, they racked up a combined 3,118 points in the regular season and another 485 in the playoffs.

When it comes to forward-defenseman duos, it's tough to top Boston's Phil Esposito and Bobby Orr. The heart and soul of the Bruins, they placed 1-2 in NHL scoring five times in six seasons from 1970-75; the only year they didn't, they were 1-3, with Orr finishing three points behind Art Ross runner-up Bobby Clarke.

Faceoff men, meanwhile, are extremely valuable to any team looking to, you know, possess the puck. And few centers have dominated the draw like Rod Brind'Amour and Ron Francis did for the Carolina Hurricanes from 1999 to 2004. On top of consistently winning the majority of their faceoffs, the pair had a penchant for winning important draws such as those in the defensive zone, on the power play or late in games.

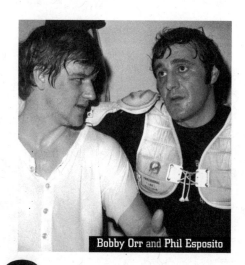

Bobby Orr and Phil Esposito

Best Venues ● ● ●

1. XCEL ENERGY CENTER, MINNESOTA
2. BELL CENTRE, MONTREAL
3. MADISON SQUARE GARDEN, NEW YORK
4. PENGROWTH SADDLEDOME, CALGARY
5. REXALL PLACE, EDMONTON
6. MELLON ARENA, PITTSBURGH
7. WACHOVIA CENTER, PHILADELPHIA
8. JOE LOUIS ARENA, DETROIT
9. RBC CENTER, CAROLINA
10. PEPSI CENTER, COLORADO

The Xcel Energy Center

It's the kind of fan experience you can only get in the Sunbelt.

Carolina Hurricanes supporters have put a southern spin on attending NHL games, getting the fun started long before the puck drops. While the players are inside doing their pre-game stretches, Canes fans are outside unlatching tailgates, firing up barbecues and enjoying a few beverages before wandering inside the RBC Center to cheer on their team.

That's when the real storm hits. Hurricanes fans are known as a raucous bunch, their defining moment coming when the RBC's entire lower bowl stood for the duration of the Canes' Stanley Cup-clinching Game 7 win over Edmonton in 2006.

The Carolina craziness began with the team's first run to the final.

"(2002) was unbelievable," said ex-Canes winger Erik Cole. "Obviously, '06 was great because we finished it off, but to see it that first time, how excited everyone was and how 'Cup Crazy' they were, I can't imagine what it would have been like if we had won it that year. It would have been absolutely insane."

Bell Centre in Montreal

Most Spectacular Rookie Seasons ● ●

1. TEEMU SELANNE
76 goals and 132 points in 1992-93, shattering rookie scoring records; first-team all-star, won Calder Trophy.

2. TONY ESPOSITO
First-team all-star, won Calder and Vezina in 1969-70; led the league in wins and set modern-day record with 15 shutouts.

3. NELS STEWART
34 goals in 36 games and led the league in scoring in 1925-26; won Hart.

4. MIKE BOSSY
53 goals in 1977-78 set a rookie record that stood until Selanne arrived; won Calder.

5. ED BELFOUR
Led the league in games played, wins and goals-against average in 1990-91; first-team all-star and won Calder and Vezina.

6. PETER STASTNY
39 goals and 109 points in 1980-81 set rookie marks for assists and points; won Calder.

7. RAY BOURQUE
65 points and plus-52 in 1979-80; won Calder and was named first-team all-star.

8. BERNIE GEOFFRION
30 goals and 54 points in 1951-52; sixth in scoring and won Calder.

9. BRIAN LEETCH
71 points, including record 23 goals by a rookie D-man, in 68 games in 1988-89; won Calder.

10. TOM BARRASSO
Named first-team all-star, won Calder and Vezina in 1983-84.

Teemu Selanne

There have been many dominant NHL freshmen over the years, so selecting the 10 greatest rookie performances of all-time is not an easy job.

And you've probably noticed a few big-name skaters not on the list. Wayne Gretzky tied Marcel Dionne with 137 points in No. 99's first NHL season in 1979-80, but missed out on the scoring title because Dionne had more goals. Gretzky was not considered a rookie by the NHL's standards because he had already played pro hockey in the WHA.

More recently, Alex Ovechkin netted 52 goals and 106 points in 2005-06, finishing third in scoring and beating Sidney Crosby for the Calder Trophy. It was a spectacular effort, but Ovechkin finished 19 points behind Joe Thornton, the year's scoring champ, and only ranks third on the all-time list for goals by a rookie (behind Teemu Selanne and Mike Bossy). As crazy as it sounds, you have to do better than that to make this list. Sure, Bernie Geoffrion made the cut despite scoring "only" 30 goals, but his Canadiens made 10 straight finals in the 1950s, winning five Cups. When you can crack that lineup and finish second in team scoring, you deserve a place on this list.

Aside from Gretzky and Ovechkin, there were some other great rookie performances that didn't make the top 10. Larry Murphy tallied 76 points in 1980-81 to
set the record for most points by a rookie defenseman. Forwards Dale Hawerchuk,
Mario Lemieux, Joe Juneau and Crosby all cracked the 100-point mark. And Joe
Nieuwendyk sniped 51 goals in 75 games as a Calgary rookie in 1987-88.

But one group of rookies deserves special attention: the Stastny brothers. In the
early 1980s, Peter, Anton and Marian all defected from the former Czechoslovakia; Peter and Anton in the summer of 1980 and older brother Marian one year
later.

Playing for the Quebec Nordiques, the Stastnys took the NHL by storm. Peter and
Anton combined for 78 goals and 194 points in 1980-81, with Peter setting rookie
records for assists (70, tied by Juneau in '92-93) and points (109, surpassed by
Selanne in '92-93) to take home the Calder Trophy. The duo also share the record
for most points in a game by a rookie with eight, a feat they both managed in the
same game. The next season, Marian scored 35 goals and 89 points, 14th all-time
on the rookie list. Together, the Stastny brothers averaged 37 goals and 94 points
as rookies.

But it doesn't end there. Peter's son Paul was also successful as a rookie. In 2006-
07, the Avalanche center placed second in Calder voting behind Evgeni Malkin and
finished the season with 78 points, good for 24th all-time. And during one stretch,
Paul registered at least one point in 20 straight games, breaking the rookie record
by three games.

The Sutters may be the first family of hockey, but the Stastnys' rookie exploits make
them the first family of NHL freshmen.

Best Major Junior ● ● ● Players

1. MARIO LEMIEUX, LAVAL, 1981-84 (QMJHL)
247 goals, 562 points in 200 regular season games; set records with 61-game point streak, 133 goals and 282 points in 1983-84.

2. GUY LAFLEUR, QUEBEC, 1969-71 (QMJHL)
233 goals, 379 points in 118 regular season games; 130 goals, 209 points and a Memorial Cup victory in 1970-71.

3. SIDNEY CROSBY, RIMOUSKI, 2003-05 (QMJHL)
120 goals, 303 points in 121 games; two-time major junior player of the year; silver and gold with Canada at two world juniors.

4. BOBBY CLARKE, FLIN FLON, 1966-69 (WCHL)
305 points in 117 regular season games; two scoring titles, the trophy was later renamed in his honor.

5. BOBBY ORR, OSHAWA, 1963-66 (OHA)
Started playing major junior at 15; 259 points in 159 games as a defenseman.

6. MIKE BOSSY, LAVAL, 1973-77 (QMJHL)
309 goals, 532 points in 261 games; most goals in major junior history.

7. BOBBY SMITH, OTTAWA, 1975-78 (OHA)
158 goals, 385 points in 187 games; 69 goals, 192 points in 1977-78 to win major junior player of the year over Gretzky.

8. PAT LAFONTAINE, VERDUN, 1982-83 (QMJHL)
Major junior player of the year in 1982-83 after notching 104 goals and 234 points, both single-season rookie records.

9. ERIC LINDROS, OSHAWA, 1989-92 (OHL)
97 goals, 216 points in 95 regular season games; a Memorial Cup; played in three world juniors; major junior player of the year in 1990-91.

10. WAYNE GRETZKY, SAULT STE. MARIE, 1977-78 (OHA)
70 goals, 182 points in 1977-78; 17 points in six games for Canada at 1978 world junior as a 16-year-old.

Choosing the top 10 major junior players of all-time is a harrowing task. The players who made the cut are widely known to hockey fans, but there are many others who could've made the list.

In the Western Hockey League, the all-time leading scorer (with 591 points) is Brian Sakic – Joe's younger brother – and Rob Brown once tallied 76 goals and 212 points in 63 games for Kamloops. In the Ontario Hockey League, Ernie Godden netted 87 goals for Windsor in 1980-81 and Bryan Fogarty put up 47 goals and 155 points in '88-89 as a defenseman. During 1973-74 in the high-flying Quebec Major Junior Hockey League, Pierre Larouche potted at least one goal in 27 straight games and finished with 251 points, second all-time only to Mario Lemieux's 282 in 1983-84.

Bobby Clarke

Of the 10 names on the list, perhaps the one who's more known for his exploits after joining the NHL than before is Bobby Clarke. Clarke was born and raised in Flin Flon, Man., a provincial border town about a 10-hour drive from Winnipeg known for bitter cold and, later, Clarke. He began playing for his hometown Flin Flon Bombers when he was eight and didn't stop until graduating to the NHL. So, in his entire life, Clarke played for just two organizations.

Despite its small population – today, Flin Flon is home to about 6,300 people – the community was once home to a major junior team, and a good one at that. Clarke played two seasons for the Bombers in the late '60s. And with future NHL 60-goal man Reggie Leach playing on his wing, Clarke and the Bombers dominated.

Clarke totaled 305 points in 117 regular season games, won two scoring titles and was named the league's player of the year in 1968-69. He also led the Bombers to two regular season titles and a league championship. Clarke was so dominant the league changed the name of the trophy awarded to its top scorer to the Bob Clarke Trophy.

But perhaps Clarke's most important function with the Bombers was not as scoring leader, but as a role model. Diagnosed with diabetes as a child, Clarke's ability to compete in the pros was questioned – because of his medical condition – as he rose through the ranks in Flin Flon from local player to junior star.

He eventually made his way to the Mayo Clinic in Minnesota, where doctors concluded he was fully capable of playing professional hockey as long as his condition was monitored. By all accounts, Clarke should have been the first overall selection in the 1969 NHL amateur draft. But fears concerning his health caused him to slip all the way to 17th, where Philadelphia snapped him up. Montreal and Detroit quickly put packages together to try and pry Clarke away from the Flyers, but to no avail.

Learning to deal with diabetes as a pro came slowly to Clarke – in his first training camp he had two diabetic seizures. But with a personal diet plan developed by Philadelphia trainer Frank Lewis, Clarke learned to control his disease. He went on to a Hall of Fame career in the NHL, but more importantly showed the world that diabetic athletes could compete and excel at the highest level.

Best •••••
Shooters

1. BRETT HULL	
2. JARI KURRI	
3. MIKE BOSSY	
4. GUY LAFLEUR	
5. TEEMU SELANNE	
6. PHIL ESPOSITO	
7. BRENDAN SHANAHAN	
8. MARIO LEMIEUX	
9. LUC ROBITAILLE	
10. GORDIE DRILLON	

Mike Bossy could shoot from anywhere, including the lip.

Proving the cocky young athlete is by no means a recent phenomenon, Bossy was very straightforward with GM Bill Torrey during their first contract negotiation after the New York Islanders had drafted the junior star 15th overall in 1977.

When Torrey's initial offer wasn't to the 20-year-old's liking, Bossy responded by saying something to the effect that it "wasn't a lot of money for a guy who would score 50 goals."

Torrey agreed, but he didn't think Bossy was going to hit that magical barrier, especially in his first NHL season.

But Bossy, who had scored 309 goals for Laval in 261 career QMJHL games, tallied 53 times in his rookie NHL season of 1977-78, setting a freshman mark that stood until Teemu Selanne's stunning 76-goal campaign in 1992-93.

Bossy went on to set a record with nine straight 50-goal seasons and his career mark of 0.76 goals per game is the highest in NHL history.

A quick release, more so than velocity or even accuracy, was Bossy's trademark.

Not all shooters have the same arsenal, but they're tied together by the fact they piled up a ton of goals with shots that aren't purely slapshots or wrist shots. Yes, Brett Hull could blast a slapshot with the best of them, but his real gift was one-timing the puck with stagger- ing accuracy. Ditto for Guy Lafleur, whose low drives to the corner of the net terror- ized goalies in the 1970s. Phil Esposito didn't have much mustard on his shots, but who had quicker hands from 10 feet out than the big Bruin?

Mike
Bossy

Best Checking ● ● ●
Forwards
Since Expansion

1. BOB GAINEY
Won the first four Selke Trophies as the NHL's top defensive forward and actually made it sexy to be a checker.

2. GUY CARBONNEAU
Another Canadiens defensive great was a fine two-way player, and extended his career by becoming a shutdown guy.

3. JOHN MADDEN
Would likely have been a better two-way threat playing for anybody other than the Devils, but he'll cherish his two (and counting) Stanley Cups regardless.

4. JERE LEHTINEN
Three-time Selke Trophy winner was a major contributor to the Dallas Stars' 1999 Stanley Cup championship.

5. DOUG JARVIS
One of the many graduates of the Roger Neilson School of Defense, Jarvis developed from a junior scoring star into an NHL ironman and defensive center.

6. ROD BRIND'AMOUR
One of the hardest workers, on and off the ice, to ever skate in the NHL, Brind'Amour is a Hall of Famer in waiting.

7. SERGEI FEDOROV
When his scoring prowess began to fade, the 1994 Hart Trophy winner continued to rely on his ability to limit the opposition's scoring chances.

8. CRAIG RAMSAY
Like his fellow Peterborough Petes graduates Gainey and Jarvis, Ramsay's calling card at the NHL level was defense – to the tune of one Selke Trophy and three runner-up finishes.

9. PAVEL DATSYUK

It has yet to be determined exactly how high he'll climb up the scoring ladder, but one thing is certain, his play without the puck ranks among the best in the NHL.

10. DOUG GILMOUR

If this gritty little center ever makes it into the Hall of Fame (he's on the bubble), it will be largely because of his dogged defensive play.

Bob Gainey was once paid the highest compliment a player could ever hope for when legendary Russian hockey coach Anatoli Tarasov called him "the most complete hockey player in the world."

At a time when Canada and Russia were waging war for world hockey supremacy, it raised Gainey's profile to the highest point of his long, illustrious career. A decent scorer in junior (he scored 22 goals in 52 games his final year of junior with his hometown team, the OHL's Peterborough Petes), it was Gainey's ability to impede others from scoring that made him famous.

Bob Gainey

In fact, when the NHL decided to honor the best defensive forward with the Frank J. Selke Trophy in 1978, Gainey won it the first four years it was awarded and then finished second in the fifth.

With a greater emphasis on scoring these days, there are some who feel the NHL is hypocritical to honor defensive forwards. But as long as the game is played, there will always be a need for teams to try to shut down the opposition's best scorers and there will always be individuals that make their greatest impact as defensive stalwarts.

Players Who ● ● ●
Should Be Coaches

1. JOHN MADDEN
Understands the value of team defense, but is one Devil who can navigate his way to the other team's net, too.

2. GLEN METROPOLIT
A survivor who beat the odds by making it back to the NHL when it looked like he was done, he understands what it takes to be a winner.

3. IAN LAPERRIERE
Grinding forward displays a passion for the game every shift he skates and is a positive influence on others.

4. ETHAN MOREAU
One of the NHL's great unheralded leaders, he commands respect from both teammates and opponents.

5. BOBBY HOLIK
A dedicated athlete with a championship pedigree, he could become the NHL's first successful European-born and -trained coach.

6. GREGORY CAMPBELL
OK, it's still pretty early in his playing career, but this kid is a dependable defense-first NHLer with coaching bloodlines.

7. CHRIS CLARK
Inspirational leader with a fine understanding of both sides of the puck.

8. JASON POMINVILLE
Blossoming offensive star knows how to play in the new NHL and is a team leader.

9. DEAN McAMMOND

Journeyman forward has battled injuries, but has also displayed excellent survival skills and leadership qualities.

10. CHRIS CHELIOS

Wouldn't it be amazing if Chelios translated his obvious passion for playing into a teaching role?

There is no exact mold for creating the perfect coach.

Some successful NHL coaches were big-time stars before they stepped behind the bench and some never made it to the big leagues at all. Many were great defensive players during their playing days, but recently there has been a trend to go with coaches who were good offensive players – Wayne Gretzky, Bruce Boudreau and John Anderson among them. What matters most is having a good game plan and being able to get your message across.

John Madden

Greatest ● ● ● ●
International Rivalries

Grudge match: **Finland** vs. **Sweden**

1. CANADA VS. SOVIET UNION/RUSSIA
Memories of the dramatic 1972 Summit Series showdown and 1987
Canada Cup make this the game's greatest rivalry.

2. SOVIET UNION VS. CZECH REPUBLIC/CZECHOSLOVAKIA
Eastern Bloc battle became a full-scale war on ice after the 1968 invasion of
Czechoslovakia by Soviet troops.

3. FINLAND VS. SWEDEN
Classic clash of Nordic neighbors highlighted by the Finns' only world
championship gold medal – a 4-1 upset of the Swedes in Stockholm in 1995.

4. CANADA VS. UNITED STATES

Upstart Amerks knocked off their Canadian rivals in 1996 World Cup;
Canucks got golden revenge at 2002 Olympics.

5. CZECH REPUBLIC VS. SLOVAKIA

Formerly united as Czechoslovakia, the two became foes on the ice
following the breakup of the country in 1993.

6. SOVIET UNION VS. UNITED STATES

American collegians' monumental upset of the Soviets at Lake Placid in 1980
was named No. 1 international hockey event by the IIHF.

7. CANADA VS. SWEDEN

Peter Forsberg's golden shootout goal at the 1994 Olympics helped the
Swedes atone for many international losses to Canada.

8. CANADA VS. FINLAND

Once one-sided series became competitive after Carl Brewer taught
the Finns some of Canada's hockey secrets.

9. GERMANY VS. SWITZERLAND

The running feud for the final spot in the top six hockey nations in
Europe reached a fever pitch when they clashed in the quarterfinals at
the 1992 world championship.

10. RUSSIA VS. LATVIA

Latvian parliament closed down to watch its boys stun the host Russians 3-2
at the 2000 world championship in St. Petersburg.

The first major blow to Canadian hockey pride was struck in 1954 when the Soviet Union, competing in the world championship for the first time, stunned Toronto's East York Lyndhursts 7-2 to win the gold medal.

Eighteen years later, Canada came to a standstill as fans gathered around their TV sets to watch Paul Henderson score the winning goal with 34 seconds left to play in the historic Summit Series, the first time the country's best NHLers faced the Soviets. The series had political overtones with Canada adopting the role of fighters for democracy against a Communist system.

The Cold War was waning, but hockey's greatest rivalry was still burning when the two countries met in the 1987 Canada Cup. With Wayne Gretzky and Mario Lemieux teaming up, Canada won the best-of-3 final series in the dying minutes. Many consider it the best hockey of all-time.

The Czechoslovakians are given credit for teaching the game to the Soviets in the 1940s, but animosity between the two countries grew over the next 20 years and peaked when Soviet troops invaded Czechoslovakia in 1968. In the next World Championship, the Czechoslovakians stunned the Soviets by beating them twice in Stockholm in 1969. Czechoslovakian fans didn't even care that their national team wound up with only a bronze medal after losing twice to Sweden; they were thrilled the Soviet team had been taught a lesson.

The Finnish-Swedish rivalry dates back to 1928 when club teams from the two countries faced off on an outdoor rink. At one time, Finland was part of Sweden and Swedish still is the official second language there. (Sweden's king conquered Finland in 1155 and it wasn't until 1809 that the countries became separate nations again.)

Although the Swedes were embarrassed in losing the world championship final on home ice to Finland in 1995, they gained a measure of revenge when the worlds were held in Helsinki in 2003. Down 5-1 to the Finns in the semifinals, the Swedes rallied to win 6-5.

Canada dominated the United States from the day the two nations first met in 1920. But with the game growing in leaps and bounds, particularly in the collegiate ranks, the Yanks finally made a breakthrough, rallying from a 2-1 third period deficit to upset Canada 5-2 in the championship game of the 1996 World Cup in Montreal. And in Finland in 2004, the U.S. national junior team staged another great comeback to knock off Canada 4-3 in the gold medal game of the world junior championship.

Best ●●●●●●
Defense Pairings

1. SCOTT STEVENS AND SCOTT NIEDERMAYER
The Devils won three Stanley Cups thanks to Niedermayer's speed and skill and Stevens' thundering open-ice hits.

2. LARRY ROBINSON AND SERGE SAVARD
Scotty Bowman called them the best blueline tandem he had ever seen.

3. DENIS POTVIN AND STEFAN PERSSON
Potent power play combo won four straight Cup championships with the Islanders.

4. BOBBY ORR AND DALLAS SMITH
Orr won eight straight Norris Trophies and Smith was plus-30 or better seven times.

5. PAUL COFFEY AND CHARLIE HUDDY
Stay-at-home Huddy and swift-skating, high-scoring Coffey complemented each other perfectly.

6. DOUG HARVEY AND BUTCH BOUCHARD
Hall of Famers formed a formidable first blueline pair for Habs in early 1950s.

7. RAY BOURQUE AND DON SWEENEY
Nos. 1 and 2 on the all-time list of games played by Boston Bruins defensemen.

8. TIM HORTON AND ALLAN STANLEY
Veteran rearguards protected Johnny Bower in Toronto's three consecutive Cup wins, 1962-64.

9. NICKLAS LIDSTROM AND LARRY MURPHY
World-class backline support for Yzerman & Co. in Detroit's Stanley Cup victories of 1997 and '98

10. SLAVA FETISOV AND ALEXEI KASATONOV
Personal enemies nevertheless combined for success with Russian national team and New Jersey Devils.

At a time when hockey was in danger of becoming a roller derby on ice, a pair of Montreal Canadiens policemen came to the rescue.

It was Larry Robinson and Serge Savard who stood up to the Philadelphia Flyers and ended the Broad Street Bullies' two-year reign as Stanley Cup champions in 1976.

And while Bobby Orr wheeled up and down the ice, leading the NHL in scoring in 1969-70, his partner Dallas Smith kept the ice clear in front of the Boston net with remarkable consistency.

Scott Niedermayer and Scott Stevens

With Martin Brodeur in goal and Scott Stevens and Scott Niedermayer in front of him, the New Jersey Devils built a fortress around their net. Stevens and Niedermayer knew each other so well that Niedermayer would often steer an attacker in Stevens' direction, where his partner was waiting to land a solid hit.

Denis Potvin won two Norris Trophies, and Stefan Persson was a steady defender and superb puckhandler who was considered a poor man's Borje Salming.

During the Edmonton Oilers' glory years in the 1980s, Charlie Huddy often stayed back to protect netminder Grant Fuhr, while Paul Coffey went on one of his patented rushes with the puck.

Doug Harvey earned seven Norris Trophies and Butch Bouchard was a three-time first-team all-star in the 1940s.

Allan Stanley was 41 and Tim Horton 37 when the pair won the last of their four Stanley Cups together in Toronto in 1967. Horton was considered one of the NHL's strongest players.

Ray Bourque led the Bruins in scoring five times; in 1999–2000, Don Sweeney had 301 hits and 84 blocked shots.

Seldom have two better offensive talents played defense together than when Nicklas Lidstrom and Larry Murphy paired up in Detroit. The result was a big boost in the Red Wings' puck-possession time and a tremendously productive power play.

Slava Fetisov and Alexei Kasatonov were part of the best five-man unit in the history of hockey. What's ironic is that the two disliked each other as a result of allegations that Kasatonov was reporting the actions of Fetisov and Igor Larionov to Soviet Red Army coach Viktor Tikhonov when Fetisov and Larionov were trying to make their break from the Soviet Union to play in the NHL.

Most ● ● ● ● ● ●
Underrated Players

1. CLAUDE PROVOST
A nine-time Stanley Cup champion, Provost didn't get the headlines like many of his teammates (Jean Beliveau, Dickie Moore, Jacques Plante, the Richard brothers, etc.), but he was an effective two-way player who led the Canadiens in scoring in 1964-65.

2. CHRIS OSGOOD
He has three Stanley Cups, two as a starter, and he deserves credit for being the backbone of a great winning organization in Detroit.

3. DALLAS SMITH
It took a while before Smith became a regular with the Boston Bruins, but once he arrived he was a stalwart on two Stanley Cup championship teams.

4. STEFAN PERSSON
Some people acted like Denis Potvin was the only defenseman on the Islanders dynasty that won four straight Cups. But Persson was a solid two-way per-former who gave the Islanders reliable secondary scoring from the blueline.

5. ED WESTFALL
Known primarily for his penalty-killing ability, Westfall was actually a decent scorer who hit the 25-goal plateau twice in an era when 25 goals meant something.

6. JEFF BEUKEBOOM
The big Lindsay, Ont., native made life easier for the more skilled players he skated with and was rewarded with four Stanley Cup rings for his efforts.

7. ULF DAHLEN
The slick Swede broke into the NHL with 29 goals for the Rangers in 1987-88 and remained one of the league's top corner men for more than 900 games.

8. BILLY CARROLL
Primarily a checker, Carroll parlayed his ability to shut down the other team's top scorers into four Stanley Cups in a seven-year career.

9. AARON WARD

The talkative defenseman happily plays a supporting role as a shutdown defender who blocks shots and delivers checks, and has done so on three championship teams.

10. GARY DORNHOEFER

Back in the day when forwards took a pounding in front of the net, Dornhoefer was the poster child for players willing to pay a price to score a goal.

When the Boston Bruins won the Stanley Cup in 1970 and '72, there was no mistaking it was on the backs of Bobby Orr and Phil Esposito. Esposito became the NHL's most dangerous scorer while Orr revolutionized the game with his legendary rushes.

But as Sidney Crosby and Evgeni Malkin found out in the 2008 Stanley Cup final, it takes a solid supporting cast to win an NHL championship. And while Orr and Esposito were the brightest stars on the Big, Bad Bruins, others such as Johnny McKenzie, Johnny Bucyk, Wayne Cashman and Gerry Cheevers did their share, too.

And there were others.

"The first year we won the Cup, I'd say Ken Hodge was our most underrated player," Esposito once said. "And when we won our second Cup, it was definitely Dallas Smith.

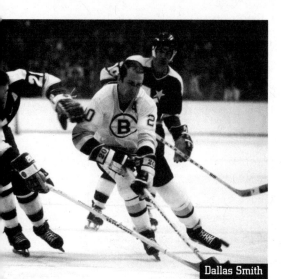
Dallas Smith

Dallas was a pretty tough guy who took care of business at our end of the rink."

Although he was never considered an enforcer, Smith was a tough guy who would drop the gloves if necessary. He played in four NHL All-Star Games and turned down an invitation to play for Team Canada at the 1972 Summit Series.

Greatest ● ● ● ●
Hockey Names

1. BEAR TRAPP
Sacred Heart Pioneers, 2005-present (NCAA)

2. LUDE CHECK
Chi, Det, 1943-45 (NHL)

3. ZARLEY ZALAPSKI
Pit, Hfd, Cgy, Mtl, Phi, 1987-2000 (NHL)

4. HNAT DOMENICHELLI
Hfd, Cgy, Atl, Min, 1996-2003 (NHL)

5. WACEY RABBIT
Providence Bruins, 2006-present (AHL)

6. PETE PEETERS
Phi, Bos, Wsh, 1978-91 (NHL)

7. PER DJOOS
Det, NYR, 1990-93 (NHL)

8. BRONCO HORVATH
NYR, Mtl, Bos, Chi, Tor, Min, 1955-68 (NHL)

9. STEELE BOOMER
Kootenay Ice, 2007-present (WHL)

10. EBBIE GOODFELLOW
Det, 1929-43 (NHL)

Good old hockey names are some of the best names you can…well, name, but these monikers are memorable for many different reasons. The diversity of the NHL is responsible for classic European names such as Per Djoos (not to mention Hakan Loob and Mikko Makela), while Canadian talents such as

Pete Peeters

Wacey Rabbit – who is named after a famous bull rider – and Hnat Domenichelli prove that unique handles are a global phenomenon.

Others on the list have names that make you wonder if they were pre-destined to play hockey; Bronco Horvath, Lude Check and Steele Boomer all scream speed and power, as do honorable mentions Butch Goring and Jeff Beukeboom.

Alliteration also keeps particular names in the public fascination, as Pete Peeters and Zarley Zalapski have proven over the years.

Yes, intriguing names have always colored the world of hockey, some as fierce as a Bear Trapp, others as kindly as a Goodfellow.

And where did the moniker Bear Trapp come from? It's not a nickname; and the former Estevan Bruin (Sask. Jr. A) and Sacred Heart Pioneer (NCAA) is technically the second to host the handle. His father, a Buffalo Sabres draftee back in the day, is Doug Bear Trapp Sr. The power forward son goes by his middle name, Bear, completing the most intimidating – and noteworthy – name in all of hockey history. So while opposing NCAA fans have been known to dress up as bears and hurl every ursine joke they can think of at Trapp, the Saskatchewan native's level of concentration is as strong as a – well, you know...

Flashes ● ● ● ●
In The Pan

1. BLAIR MACDONALD (EDM, VAN, 1977-83)

Wayne Gretzky's original linemate in Edmonton, he scored 70 goals in his first two seasons – and then just 21 more times.

2. JIM CAREY (WSH, BOS, STL, 1994-99)

Played only one more full NHL season after winning Vezina Trophy with Washington at age 22.

3. WARREN YOUNG (MIN, PIT, DET, 1982-88)

Potted 40 goals skating with Mario Lemieux in '84-85 and 22 with Detroit in '85-86, then dropped to eight in '86-87...and zero in '87-88.

4. ANDY AITKENHEAD (NYR, 1932-35)

Career minor league goalie beat Toronto in 1932-33 Stanley Cup final.

5. DMITRI KVARTALNOV (BOS, 1992-94)

Russian sniper had 30 goals and 72 points in 73 games with Boston in 1992-93, but played just 39 more NHL games.

6. STEVE PENNEY (MTL, WIN, 1984-88)

Montreal playoff hero in '84 was supplanted by Patrick Roy in Habs net.

7. NIKOLAI BORSCHEVSKY (TOR, CGY, DAL, 1992-96)

Leafs' 34-goal rookie couldn't sustain constant pounding in NHL.

8. KJELL DAHLIN (MTL, 1985-88)

Stanley Cup ring small consolation for early NHL departure.

9. CHRIS VALENTINE (WSH, 1981-84)

Great skill, but not enough size to prolong NHL career.

10. KEN HODGE JR. (BOS, TB, 1990-93)

Dad's shoes were too big to fill in Beantown.

Jim Carey

Playing on a line with Wayne Gretzky in Edmonton's first NHL season, Blair MacDonald finished 10th in league scoring in 1979-80 with 46 goals and 94 points. But when Mark Messier, Glenn Anderson and Jari Kurri arrived, MacDonald was traded to Vancouver, his career went south and he was released. He finished his playing days in Europe

Jim Carey was the NHL's first-team all-star goalie and Vezina Trophy winner with the Capitals in 1996, but he was traded to Boston and never played at the same level again. He retired in 1999 at the age of 24 after suffering an injury while playing in the minors.

In 1984-85, Warren Young, a graduate of Michigan, played on a line with second-year superstar Mario Lemieux. Young scored 40 goals in his first full NHL season and made the league's all-rookie team, but then signed a free agent contract with Detroit and would never again hit those totals. Within two years, he was out of the NHL entirely.

Andy Aitkenhead (great name for a goalie) took over the starting job in New York from John Ross Roach, but after two solid seasons with the Rangers, he lost it to Davey Kerr in 1934-35 and spent the rest of his career back in the minors. Kerr won the Vezina Trophy in 1940.

Dmitri Kvartalnov had at least one point in his first 14 NHL games, a league record, and collected 30 goals as a 26-year-old rookie. But he split the next season between Boston and Providence (AHL) and then decided to go to Europe to play, never to return to the NHL.

Canadiens coach Jacques Lemaire recalled Steve Penney from the AHL just in time for the 1984 post-season and the young goalie won nine straight playoff games, three of them by shutouts. The next season, he made the NHL all-rookie team. But he lost his starting job to Patrick Roy in 1985-86, was traded to Winnipeg, wound up in the minors and hung up his pads in 1988.

Nikolai Borschevsky had a smashing NHL debut with the Toronto Maple Leafs in 1992-93 after winning a gold medal with the Unified Team at the 1992 Olympics. He scored 34 goals as a rookie and notched the winner in overtime of Game 7 in a first round series against Detroit. But injuries caught up with him – including having his spleen removed after absorbing a big hit along the boards – and he spent most of the rest of his career in Europe, where he won a Russian League scoring title with Spartak in 1996-97.

After leading all NHL rookies in scoring – with 32 goals and 71 points – and earning a Stanley Cup ring in 1986, Kjell Dahlin ran into injury troubles in his sophomore season and he eventually returned to Sweden after playing parts of only three years in North America.

Chris Valentine recorded 30 goals and 67 points in his first 60 NHL games with Washington in 1981-82. But his production slipped after that and he left for Europe, where he had a successful 12-year career with Dusseldorf in the German League; he led the loop in scoring seven times.

The son of Ken Hodge Sr., who played on a legendary line in Boston with Phil Esposito and Wayne Cashman in the 1970s, Ken Hodge Jr. made the NHL all-rookie team playing alongside Cam Neely and scored 30 goals in '90-91. But he was an average skater and not as talented as his father, and wound up bouncing around the minors and playing in Great Britain.

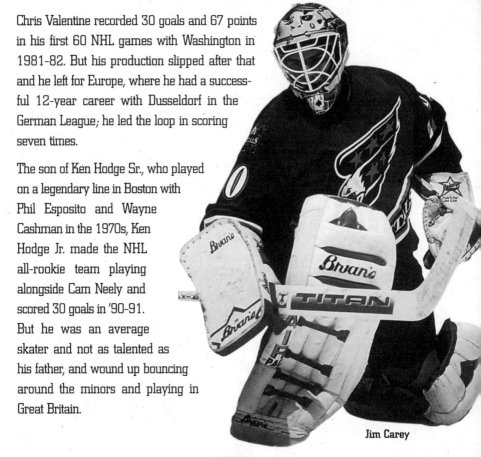

Jim Carey

Most Surprising ● ● ●
Playoff Performances
By A Goalie Since Expansion

1. KEN DRYDEN, Montreal, 1971
Won Stanley Cup and Conn Smythe Trophy

2. PATRICK ROY, Montreal, 1986
Won Stanley Cup and Conn Smythe Trophy

3. CAM WARD, Carolina, 2006
Won Stanley Cup and Conn Smythe Trophy

4. RON HEXTALL, Philadelphia, 1987
Won Conn Smythe Trophy

5. BILL RANFORD, Edmonton, 1990
Won Stanley Cup and Conn Smythe Trophy

6. STEVE PENNEY, Montreal, 1984
Lost in Game 6 of conference final

7. SEAN BURKE, New Jersey, 1988
Lost in Game 7 of conference final

8. JOHAN HEDBERG, Pittsburgh, 2001
Lost in Game 5 of conference final

9. J-S GIGUERE, Anaheim, 2003
Won Conn Smythe Trophy

10. RICHARD BRODEUR, Vancouver, 1982
Lost to Islanders in Stanley Cup final

Montreal is a city soaked in hockey tradition. One of the more curious Habs conventions is planning parades based on the shocking performance of a previously unknown goalie.

Ken Dryden

Ken Dryden had played all of six games in the NHL when he turned in a spring for the ages in 1971. First, the gangly 6-foot-4 stopper almost single-handedly eliminated the heavily favored Boston Bruins in a stunning seven-game upset in Round 1. Montreal, which had missed the playoffs for the first time in 22 years the previous season, eventually went on to defeat the Chicago Black Hawks in another seven-game series in the Stanley Cup final. Dryden, who posted a 12-8 record in the playoffs, was named Conn Smythe Trophy winner as post-season MVP. In the strangest bit of hardware chronology imaginable, he went on the claim the Calder Trophy as the NHL's rookie of the year in the following season.

Fifteen years later, history essentially repeated itself when a fresh-faced kid named Patrick Roy led a young Montreal team to an unlikely Stanley Cup in 1986. Compared to Dryden's half-dozen games, Roy's 48 contests' worth of NHL experience before his big run seems like a lifetime of preparation. But while Dryden was just a few months shy of his 24th birthday in May of '71, Roy was only 20 years old when he posted a 15-5 record and a 1.92 goals-against average in leading the Habs to their 23rd championship. Like Dryden, Roy was handed the Conn Smythe Trophy for his troubles and remains the youngest recipient of the award in league history.

Two years before Roy blasted onto the scene, Steve Penney came out of nowhere to put a charge into Canadiens fans during the spring of 1984. While the glass skate shattered in the conference final versus the four-time defending Cup-champion Islanders, Penney's play helped the Habs squeeze out a six-game victory in the Battle of Quebec in Round 2, following a victory over Boston in the first round. Unlike Dryden and Roy, Penney's explosive playoff debut wasn't the start of a long, Hall of Fame career. After a moderately successful season the following year in 1984-85, Penney played a grand total of 33 more NHL games with Montreal and the Winnipeg Jets before retiring.

Two Conn Smythe winners – Ron Hextall and Jean-Sebastien Giguere – probably enquired about trading up after they received their awards. Both goalies, in their inaugural post-season showings, came within one win of leading their team to a championship.

As a rookie in 1987, Hextall helped the Philadelphia Flyers claw back from a 3-1 series deficit in the Cup final and force a Game 7 versus the high-flying Edmonton Oilers. While Edmonton took the series with a 3-1 win in the decisive contest, Hextall announced his presence to the world by posting a 2.77 GAA in what was then a much more high-scoring league. Hextall also provided a glimpse into his nasty side when he viciously hacked Oilers center Kent Nilsson on the back of the leg during the final, earning himself an eight-game suspension to start the next season.

Giguere was the most important Duck on the frozen pond when an ultra-defensive Anaheim team lost a seven-game final to New Jersey in 2003. The playoff newbie posted five shutouts and a microscopic 1.62 GAA that year, but, alas, one less win than he wanted. Giguere, unlike Hextall, eventually did get his ring when the Ducks won the Cup in 2007.

Best●●●●●●
Playoff Beards

1. LANNY McDONALD
2. SCOTT NIEDERMAYER
3. KEN MORROW
4. MIKE COMMODORE
5. CLARK GILLIES
6. RANDY GREGG
7. JASON SMITH
8. KEN DANEYKO
9. PETER FORSBERG
10. DAVE LOWRY

Mike Commodore

Part superstition, part solidarity, the play-off beard is a tradition unique to hockey.

It's believed the New York Islanders dynasty in the early 1980s started the scruffy tradition of putting down the razor until your team either wins the Stanley Cup or is eliminated. The likes of Ken Morrow, Denis Potvin, Clark Gillies and Butch Goring all sported the rugged look while winning four consecutive Cups.

Modern-day grizzly bears Mike Commodore and Scott Niedermayer have gained recent notoriety for their distinct versions of the playoff beard.

Commodore became something of a cult hero during Calgary's run to the Cup final in 2004. Not only did he grow out his fire-red beard, the big defenseman also let his curly hair get unruly, prompting some to wonder whether the Flames had Ronald McDonald patrolling the back end. Commodore reprised his red ritual during Carolina's charge to the 2006 title.

The McDonald who long ago set the bar for facial hair in Calgary was Lanny McDonald, whose walrus moustache was on display for all to see – joined by a thick beard – after the Flames won the 1989 championship.

Niedermayer, meanwhile, looked to be equal parts lumberjack and professor with his mature, untrimmed

Denis Potvin

'salt and pepper' beard during Anaheim's Cup win in 2007. His brother, Rob, also got in on the act by growing his own winning whiskers.

Best •••••
Hockey Faces

1. BOBBY CLARKE
2. MIKE RICCI
3. MAURICE RICHARD
4. TIM HUNTER
5. TERRY SAWCHUK
6. BOBBY HULL
7. DOUG GILMOUR
8. TIGER WILLIAMS
9. ALEX OVECHKIN
10. BORJE SALMING

They're the guys with faces only a coach could love.

What could be more hockey than a gap-toothed Bobby Clarke grinning ear-to-ear while standing beside the Stanley Cup in a moment of pure playoff essence? Or how about Tim Hunter's nose, which always looked like it just lost a fight with a puck?

One of hockey's most enduring headshots is the picture of Jacques Plante, face and jersey bloodied by an Andy Bathgate slapshot, pulling a mask over his mangled mug.

When Borje Salming first landed in North America, players were determined to run the Swede right out of the rink with intense – and often dirty – physical play. But Salming survived the ordeal en route to NHL stardom, and his toughness was validated forever when he was left looking like Frankenstein after Detroit's Gerard Gallant accidentally stepped on his face during a goalmouth scramble. It took 300 stitches to sew Salming back together.

These days, a new batch of NHL faces has emerged despite advances in dental practices and plastic surgery. Alex Ovechkin lost one of his front teeth while playing basketball, but the fact he didn't immediately replace it gives him a look that is quintessentially hockey.

Of course, faces don't always have to be known for their rougher characteristics. Bobby Hull may have been the first player to sign a million-dollar contract, but The Golden Jet gained notoriety long before that at least partially because of his million-dollar smile.

Bobby Clarke

Best ●●●●●
Hockey Movies

1. SLAP SHOT (1977)
2. MIRACLE (2004)
3. THE ROCKET (2005)
4. NET WORTH (1995)
5. THE SWEATER (1980)
6. BON COP, BAD COP (2006)
7. LES CHIEFS (2004)
8. THE RHINO BROTHERS (2001)
9. MYSTERY, ALASKA (1999)
10. YOUNGBLOOD (1986)

Though the pool of hockey films is not a deep one, the game has inspired a collection of must-see movies. At the top of the list is the cult classic *Slap Shot*, which has stood the test of time and remains a must-watch on minor hockey bus trips. The slapstick comedy with classic one-liners has entertained generations of hockey fans. The Hanson brothers – David Hanson and Steve and Jeff Carlson – are still making a living off the movie (which spawned an awful sequel in 2002).

Then there's *Miracle*, the story of a mish-mash team of college players led by legendary coach Herb Brooks, who took on and defeated the Soviet Union at the 1980 Olympics in one of the biggest upsets in hockey history.

Another fine hockey film is *The Rocket*. An award-winning biography of Montreal Canadiens legend Maurice Richard, it tells the tale of a young machinist turned hockey superstar during a period of social unrest in French-speaking Canada.

SLAP SHOT

Made in the mid-'90s, *Net Worth* is the adaptation of David Cruise's book about Ted Lindsay's quest to create a player's union to protect the rights of the players against the owners. The story has been called "the bloodiest fight in the history of the NHL not to take place on the ice."

And don't forget the cartoon adaptation of Roch Carrier's *The Sweater*. It's the 1950s tale of a young Canadiens fan in small-town Quebec who receives a Maple Leafs jersey instead of the jersey of his idol Maurice Richard.

As for the 1990s *Mighty Ducks* trilogy, there are two schools of thought: Yes, the Disney movies are significant because they introduced hockey to a generation of American children and spurred the arrival of the NHL in Anaheim, but on the other hand, they were pure Hollywood schlock. Check out *Net Worth* or *Les Chiefs* for a more worthwhile cinematic experience.

Stompin' Tom Connors

••Best Hockey Songs

1. THE HOCKEY THEME (LONGTIME HOCKEY NIGHT IN CANADA THEME SONG)
Dolores Claman

2. THE HOCKEY SONG
Stompin' Tom Connors

3. FIFTY-MISSION CAP
The Tragically Hip

4. GRETZKY ROCKS
The Pursuit of Happiness

5. BIG LEAGUE
Tom Cochrane

6. (I FEEL LIKE GERRY) CHEEVERS (GOT STITCH MARKS ON MY HEART)
Chixdiggit!

7. HOCKEY
Jane Siberry

8. THE BALLAD OF WENDEL CLARK PARTS 1 AND 2
The Rheostatics

9. HELMET SONG
The Zambonis

10. THE ZAMBONI SONG
Gear Daddies

Saturday night will never be the same. That was the sentiment among hockey fans in Canada when it was announced in the summer of 2008 that CBC no longer held the rights to the song that kicked off every *Hockey Night in Canada* broadcast for the past 40 years.

Known to many as Canada's second national anthem, *The Hockey Theme* was the opening music for the oldest running sports program in the history of television. But when CBC refused to pay the licensing fee demanded by Dolores Claman, who composed the song in 1968, CTV swooped in and secured the rights to the track.

The famous jingle is the mental soundtrack to every hockey game played in Canada, whether it's on the road, pond or indoor ice. The song has transcended generations of hockey fans and is easily the greatest hockey song ever composed.

A close second is Stompin' Tom Connors' *The Hockey Song*. Though it originally appeared on Connors' 1973 album, *Stompin' Tom and the Hockey Song,* the track didn't achieve popularity until 1992 when Pat Burns, coach of the Toronto Maple Leafs, took a liking to the tune and had it played during home games at Maple Leaf Gardens. These days, you'd be hard-pressed to sit through an NHL game without hearing Connors croon, "Hello out there/we're on the air/it's hockey night tonight."

The Tragically Hip's *Fifty-Mission Cap* describes the mysterious disappearance of Maple Leafs defenseman Bill Barilko, who scored the Stanley Cup-clinching goal over the Montreal Canadiens in 1951. Barilko went home to Timmins, Ont., and, after deciding to go on a fishing trip, he boarded a small, single-engine plane that disappeared somewhere over Northern Ontario. The Leafs then endured the longest Stanley Cup drought in franchise history to that point, only to win their next championship in 1962, the same year Barilko's body was discovered.

Best Coaches ● ● ● ●
Who Never Played
in the NHL

1. SCOTTY BOWMAN

9 Stanley Cups

2. TOMMY IVAN

3 Stanley Cups

3. PUNCH IMLACH

4 Stanley Cups

4. ROGER NEILSON

0 Stanley Cups

5. PAT BURNS

1 Stanley Cup

6. KEN HITCHCOCK

1 Stanley Cup

7. MIKE KEENAN

1 Stanley Cup

8. HERB BROOKS

0 Stanley Cups

9. HARRY SINDEN

1 Stanley Cup

10. BRYAN MURRAY

0 Stanley Cups

Were it not for a head injury in junior hockey, Scotty Bowman may never have become one of the greatest minds in NHL history. The bench boss for a record nine Stanley Cups (with three different teams) never suited up in the NHL before stepping behind the bench for St. Louis in 1967. Amazingly, Bowman had only coached in the minors before guiding the fledgling Blues to the Stanley Cup final in the franchise's first three seasons. In 1971, he was hired to take over the Montreal Canadiens and his legacy truly began to take shape as he won five Cups in eight years.

The NHL has hosted many coaches who had no experience as players in the game's best league, especially recently, and their teams didn't suffer for it. Mike Babcock, Bob Hartley and Ken Hitchcock are just three examples of the talent that comes from non-NHL backgrounds.

Back in the Original Six days, a coach could find work even if he hadn't been through the NHL wars himself. Punch Imlach went from a center on the senior league Quebec Aces to player-coach to coach before guiding the Toronto Maple Leafs to four Stanley Cups, while legendary Detroit Red Wings coach Tommy Ivan stopped playing hockey after breaking his cheekbone in a senior league prior to the Second World War. Ivan even became a referee before eventually finding his way to three Cups in the Motor City in the 1950s. At the time, Ivan was the only NHL coach who had not played in the league.

Scotty Bowman

Even one of the greatest coaching performances ever came from a man who had never laced 'em up on *Hockey Night in Canada*. In 1980, American Olympic coach Herb Brooks took a ragtag bunch of kids from Minnesota and Boston-area college teams and turned the hockey world upside-down with a semifinal victory over the Soviets – followed by a win over Finland for the gold medal – at Lake Placid. Naturally, Brooks had some insight into the international game; he had played for Team USA in two Olympics and five world championships before moving on to coach the University of Minnesota to prominence in the 1970s.

Some of the game's great innovators also never played at the highest level. Perhaps a lack of on-ice acumen was the reason Roger Neilson took up the practice of watching so much game video. If Neilson had any visions of playing in an NHL arena, he certainly snuffed them out quickly; his first coaching gig came while he was a 17-year-old student at McMaster University in Hamilton, Ont. Working his way up from coaching kids to men, Neilson was one of the most memorable skippers in the game's history.

Another one of the game's great drill sergeants came from the most disciplined of disciplines: Pat Burns was a police officer in Montreal before making his mark as coach of the Habs, Leafs and Bruins before heading the Stanley Cup-winning New Jersey Devils.

Most ● ● ● ●
Traveled Players

1. MIKE SILLINGER
12 teams (Det, Ana, Van, Phi, TB, Fla, Ott, CBJ, Phx, StL, Nsh, NYI);
1,042 games (1991-present)

2. J-J DAIGNEAULT
10 teams (Van, Phi, Mtl, StL, Pit, Ana, NYI, Nsh, Phx, Min); 899 games (1984-2001)

3. MICHEL PETIT
10 teams (Van, NYR, Que, Tor, Cgy, LA, TB, Edm, Phi, Phx); 827 games (1982-98)

4. PAUL COFFEY
9 teams (Edm, Pit, LA, Det, Hfd, Phi, Chi, Car, Bos); 1,049 games (1980-2001)

5. GRANT LEDYARD
9 teams (NYR, LA, Bos, Wsh, Buf, Dal, Van, Ott, TB); 1,028 games (1984-2002)

6. BRENT ASHTON
9 teams (Van, Col, NJ, Min, Que, Det, Wpg, Wsh, Cgy); 998 games (1979-93)

7. BRYAN MARCHMENT
9 teams (Wpg, Chi, Hfd, Edm, TB, SJ, Col, Tor, Cgy); 926 games (1988-2006)

8. JIM McKENZIE
9 teams (Hfd, Dal, Pit, Wpg, Phx, Ana, Wsh, NJ, Nsh); 880 games (1989-2004)

9. TONY HRKAC
9 teams (StL, Que, SJ, Chi, Dal, Edm, NYI, Ana, Atl); 758 games (1987-2003)

10. BOBBY DOLLAS
9 teams (Wpg, Que, Det, Ana, Edm, Pit, Ott, Cgy, SJ); 645 games (1985-2001)

There was a time, a decade or two ago, when it wasn't uncommon for NHL players to play with one team for their entire career. Two or three teams was the norm, and if you played for four or more clubs over the course of your career, they started calling you 'Suitcase'. Brent Ashton, for example, became 'Boxcar' in the 1980s as he traveled across North America from one NHL team to another. In all, Ashton suited up for nine clubs and was the standard to which all other "well-traveled" players were compared.

Mike Sillinger

With the advent of free agency and explosion of player salaries in the 1990s, movement became more common and more acceptable. Players held out and forced trades, or skipped from one short-term free agency deal to another – or, as was the case in the old days, they were good enough to appear attractive to one team, but not quite good enough to convince their current team to keep them.

Mike Sillinger has taken over as the NHL's travelin' man of the 21st century, having played for an even dozen teams. He's under contract to the Islanders in 2008-09 – but don't be surprised if he gets traded to team No. 13.

In all, 111 players have skated for seven or more NHL teams.

Best NHL ●●●●
Family Acts

1. THE SUTTERS
brothers Brian, Darryl, Duane, Brent, Rich and Ron (and sons Brandon and Brett)

2. THE RICHARDS
brothers Maurice and Henri

3. THE HULLS
brothers Bobby and Dennis and son Brett

4. THE HOWES
father Gordie and sons Mark and Marty

5. THE MAHOVLICHS
brothers Frank and Peter

6. THE ESPOSITOS
brothers Phil and Tony

7. THE STASTNYS
brothers Peter, Anton and Marian and sons Paul and Yan

8. THE PATRICKS
brothers Lester and Frank, sons Lynn and Muzz and grandsons Craig and Glenn

9. THE CONACHERS
brothers Charlie, Lionel and Roy and sons Brian and Pete

10. THE STAALS
brothers Eric, Marc and Jordan (and Jared)

Hockey is a family sport. Players are often said to have inherited their skills from "good bloodlines." In total, 47 pairs of brothers have played together on the same team; among them, 10 have won the Stanley Cup together, most recently Scott and Rob Niedermayer with the Anaheim Ducks in 2007. Brothers have also

Louis Sutter surrounded by his sons (L–R) **Duane**, **Rich**, **Ron** and **Brent**

squared off against each other five times in the Stanley Cup final. The Niedermayers were also the last to do so in 2003, when Scott played for New Jersey and Rob for Anaheim.

Twenty-six sons have followed in their fathers' footsteps and played for the same team. Only once has a father played with his sons in the NHL, though. Gordie Howe skated with both Mark and Marty for one season with the Hartford Whalers (as well as with the Houston Aeros in the WHA).

The Montreal Canadiens take the cake with 15 family acts having suited up for the *bleu, blanc et rouge*: nine sets of brothers, two father-son combinations, one grandfather-grandson combo, one uncle-nephew pair, one set of brother-in-laws and one combination of father-in-law and son-in-law (Howie Morenz and Bernie Geoffrion, who have gone on to see two more generations of Geoffrions reach the pro ranks, Danny and son Blake).

Honorable mentions include the Niedermayers; the Steens (father Thomas, son Alex); the Apps clan (Syl Sr., Syl Jr., Syl III and Gillian); and, some little-known pairings such as cousins Shane Doan and Carey Price, Jeff Beukeboom and Joe Nieuwendyk, and Wendel Clark, Joe Kocur and Barry Melrose.

Best Scouts ● ● ●

1. BARRY FRASER

Along with scout Lorne Davis, Fraser was instrumental in the Oilers dynasty by finding the likes of Jari Kurri, Glenn Anderson, Paul Coffey, Esa Tikkanen, Grant Fuhr and Kevin Lowe.

2. NEIL SMITH

He went on to win a Stanley Cup with the Rangers, but not before overseeing a scouting department in Detroit that selected Mike Sillinger, Bob Boughner, Nicklas Lidstrom, Sergei Fedorov and Vladimir Konstantinov in the 1989 draft. Best draft ever.

3. JIM NILL

The former journeyman NHLer heads up a Red Wings scouting department that has unearthed the likes of Henrik Zetterberg, Pavel Datsyuk, Jiri Hudler, Valtteri Filppula, Johan Franzen and Darren Helm after the 50th pick.

4. WREN BLAIR

The Boston Bruins scout camped outside the home of Doug Orr and convinced him to send his son, Bobby, to the Bruins-sponsored Oshawa Generals in the mid-'60s.

5. PAUL HAYNES

While recovering from an injury in 1939, the Canadiens sent him on a western Canada scouting trip where he unearthed Elmer Lach and Ken Reardon.

6. BOB DAVIDSON

The former Maple Leafs star had connections in Northern Ontario that allowed him to build a Stanley Cup dynasty in the 1950s comprised heavily of players from Kirkland Lake, Timmins and Sudbury.

7. DOUG ROBINSON

Presiding over a scouting staff that selected Petr Svoboda, Shayne Corson, Stephane Richer and Patrick Roy (as well as Sidney Crosby's dad, Troy) in 1984 goes a long way.

8. RUSS McCRORY

In 1943, McCrory convinced Ab and Katherine Howe to allow their son to attend a New York Rangers camp in Winnipeg. Too bad Gordie became homesick and went home, only to sign later with the Red Wings.

9. DAVID CONTE

The former college star and European league journeyman is largely responsible for the Devils landing Martin Brodeur, Sergei Brylin, Brian Rafalski, Scott Gomez, John Madden and Jay Pandolfo.

10. JACK HUMPHRIES

A Rangers scout in the 1950s and '60s, Humphries convinced Rod Gilbert and Jean Ratelle to leave Quebec to play for the Rangers-sponsored Guelph Biltmores.

Barry Fraser is not in the Hall of Fame as a builder, but he did build the Edmonton Oilers dynasty through the draft with a motherlode of Hall of Fame players.

Only four times in history has a team managed to select two Hall of Fame players in the same draft. Fraser, who was director of player personnel for the Oilers from their World Hockey Association days in 1978 through to 2000 and oversaw their drafting efforts in those years, managed to do it twice. What makes it even more impressive was that he did it in successive seasons and made the Oilers the only team in NHL history to draft Hall of Famers in three consecutive years.

In their first-ever NHL draft in 1979, Fraser selected Mark Messier 48th overall and Glenn Anderson 69th. (That came after he took Kevin Lowe 21st.) The next year, he took Paul Coffey sixth overall and Jari Kurri 69th, then drafted Grant Fuhr eighth overall in 1981.

The only other teams to get two Hall of Famers in the same year were the Montreal Canadiens in 1971 (Guy Lafleur first and Larry Robinson 20th) and the New York Islanders in 1974 (Clark Gillies fourth and Bryan Trottier 22nd). The Detroit Red Wings might make it a fifth time with their 1989 draft when they took Nicklas Lidstrom 53rd and Sergei Fedorov 74th.

Jim Nill

"They were all great players, but they're all good people, that's one thing I can say about them all," Fraser said. "There's six of them now in the Hall of Fame and the reason they're there is first of all they were great players and second of all they're great people."

While many teams were ignoring Europe, the Oilers were doing extensive scouting there, largely because of their WHA days. That league opened Europe up to North American professional hockey far earlier than the NHL did and it was Fraser's work for the Oilers in the WHA that landed them Kurri in 1980.

During the 1978-79 season, the Oilers played an exhibition game against Jokerit of the Finnish Elite League and an 18-year-old Kurri was one of the players for Jokerit. Kurri was part of the Finnish Olympic team in 1980, but received almost no ice time and scouts didn't have much of a book on him.

"With guys like Kurri and (Esa) Tikkanen, I don't think too many teams paid much attention to Finland in those days," Fraser said. "It was all Sweden."

Like any scout, Fraser has a number of skeletons in his closet when it comes to drafting players. In fact, Fraser has several wardrobes full of them with the Oilers' performance at the draft in the late 1980s and 1990s. But his early drafts were so spectacular that he is remembered as one of the best, if not the best, of all-time. Fraser always had strong scouting staffs, including Lorne Davis, who had worked for the Oilers since their NHL inception until passing away in December of 2007.

Fraser retired in 2000 and lives in Cabo San Lucas, Mexico – not exactly a breeding ground for NHL players.

"Now I only see them when they're on vacation," he said.

Players Who Should ● ●
Be In The Hall Of Fame

1. PAVEL BURE
His creative flair and finishing ability made him the game's top marksman.

2. DOUG GILMOUR
More than 1,400 points and a stretch as the game's best player.

3. DINO CICCARELLI
His 608 goals are the most among players eligible for the Hall.

4. PHIL HOUSLEY
No. 2 among U.S.-born scorers, fourth among 11 NHL defensemen.

5. BORIS MIKHAILOV
Nine world titles and two Olympic golds as a Russian leader.

Doug
Gilmour

6. GUY CARBONNEAU
The game's top shutdown forward for a decade.

7. CLAUDE LEMIEUX
Won four Cups and a Conn Smythe as a productive pest.

8. SERGEI MAKAROV
The Wayne Gretzky equivalent in Russia for many years.

9. ADAM OATES
One of the game's greatest playmakers; sixth in all-time assists.

10. ANATOLI FIRSOV
Widely considered one of the greatest Russian players ever.

There has been a trend towards global warming at the Hall of Fame in recent years.

With the Cold War between Russia and the western world long expired, the Hall of Fame has been getting in on the act with the inclusion of two Russian players, Viacheslav Fetisov in 2001 and Igor Larionov in 2008. Although Fetisov and Larionov had respectable careers in the NHL after arriving in 1989 at the ages of 31 and 28, their inductions into the hallowed shrine were due largely to their accomplishments on the ice in the former Soviet Union.

The Hall's selection committee had been very slow to recognize European players – remember, it's the *Hockey* Hall of Fame, not the *NHL* Hall of Fame – but is finally making inroads. Strangely though, the first Russian to be inducted, goaltender Vladislav Tretiak in 1989, was lauded mainly for his well-publicized participation in the 1972 Summit Series between Canada and the Soviet Union. Tretiak wasn't particularly sharp in that series, but did have a solid career in his homeland and was among the first players to embrace the western culture.

With that as a backdrop, the Hall's selection committee simply could not overlook the accomplishments of Fetisov and Larionov. They were clearly two of the most dominant players on the planet for an extended period, even though they weren't in the NHL. So it's only natural to surmise the Hall will eventually recognize the likes of Boris Mikhailhov, Sergei Makarov and Anatoli Firsov in the coming years. They also were three of the greatest Russian players ever, although only Makarov spent any time playing in the NHL.

There has to be some irony in the fact that the best player not in the Hall of Fame is a Russian who played his entire pro career in North America. That's Pavel Bure. (Remember, a player has to be retired three full seasons before becoming eligible for the Hall. That's why players such as Brett Hull, Steve Yzerman, Brian Leetch, Luc Robitaille and Alexander Mogilny are not on this list. They represent the cream of the crop for the 2009 induction.)

Bure was the game's most electrifying 1-on-1 player for a decade and was an accomplished finisher with two 60-goal seasons to his credit – and seasons of 59 and 58 goals as well. In an era when Wayne Gretzky, Mario Lemieux and Jaromir Jagr were taking turns winning scoring titles, defenders and goalies still feared Bure the most. His 437 goals in 702 regular season games represents a goals-per-game average of .623, third-best all-time behind Mike Bossy (.762) and Lemieux (.754).

One explanation as to why Bure is not in the Hall of Fame is because he didn't play long enough. He was forced into retirement at age 31 due to chronic injury issues. But the fact remains, Pat LaFontaine was inducted in 2003 with 865 games played, Cam Neely was inducted in 2005 with 726 games played and Bobby Orr was inducted in 1979 with 657 games played. They were all outstanding players whose careers were cut short by injuries.

Unbeatable ● ● ●
Streaks

1. GLENN HALL, 503 CONSECUTIVE STARTS
And Mr. Goalie never once wore a mask.

2. WAYNE GRETZKY, 51-GAME POINT STREAK
He opened the 1983-84 season on fire, averaging three points a game
(61 goals, 153 points) during 'The Streak.'

3. MONTREAL CANADIENS, FIVE CONSECUTIVE STANLEY CUPS
This looks impossible in today's 30-team NHL.

4. WAYNE GRETZKY, EIGHT CONSECUTIVE HART TROPHIES
You can't spell Gretzky without M-V-P.

5. DOUG JARVIS, 964 CONSECUTIVE GAMES
From Oct. 8, 1975, to Oct. 10, 1987, Jarvis didn't miss a single game,
making him hockey's Cal Ripken Jr.

6. BOBBY ORR, EIGHT CONSECUTIVE NORRIS TROPHIES
They should rename the trophy after this guy.

7. MONTREAL CANADIENS, 10 CONSECUTIVE OVERTIME WINS IN THE PLAYOFFS
Unfathomable 1993 Cup run buoyed by clutch victories.

8. PITTSBURGH PENGUINS, 17 CONSECUTIVE WINS
Lemieux returns from Hodgkin's disease to lead his team on all-time hot streak.

9. PHILADELPHIA FLYERS, 35-GAME UNDEFEATED STREAK
Flyers go nearly half a season without a loss in 1979-80 (25-0-10);
it's the longest such streak in North American pro sports.

10. BOSTON BRUINS, 29 CONSECUTIVE PLAYOFF APPEARANCES
The B's qualify for the post-season every year from 1968 to 1996,
then finish last in 1997 – and draft Joe Thornton No. 1 overall.

Hockey is a game of great streaks. Getting hot at the right time can be the difference between post-season play and hitting the links or winning the scoring race and finishing a forgettable second.

Wayne Gretzky holds the most impressive streak of all. In 1983-84, he scored at least one point in the first 51 games of the season. What makes this mark even more amazing is that he racked up 153 points in the run, en route to an astounding 205-point campaign.

While personal streaks are benchmarks for all-time greatness, team streaks are perhaps more challenging as it takes a number of components working in rhythm to keep a run intact.

The Pittsburgh Penguins won 17 games in a row during a time when ties still existed. Mario Lemieux had missed a chunk of the 1992-93 season after being diagnosed with Hodgkin's disease, but returned to lead his team into the playoffs on the highest of notes. A record that is just about as impressive is Pittsburgh's cross-state rivals from Philadelphia going 35 consecutive games without losing, tying 10 times in the process, in 1979-80.

The most impressive team record, though, is the Montreal Canadiens' five straight Stanley Cup championships in the late '50s.

Wayne
Gretzky

Best Late-Round ● ● ●
European Draft Picks

1. DOMINIK HASEK
207th overall, 1983, Chicago

2. PAVEL BURE
113th overall, 1989, Vancouver

3. DANIEL ALFREDSSON
133rd overall, 1994, Ottawa

4. HENRIK ZETTERBERG
210th overall, 1999, Detroit

5. SLAVA FETISOV
150th overall, 1983, New Jersey

6. PETER BONDRA
156th overall, 1990, Washington

7. IGOR LARIONOV
214th overall, 1985, Vancouver

8. PAVEL DATSYUK
171st overall, 1998, Detroit

9. EVGENI NABOKOV
219th overall, 1994, San Jose

10. TOMAS KABERLE
204th overall, 1996, Toronto

Scouting European talent has always been a tricky task. From the secrecy of the Cold War-era Soviet Union to the plethora of raw prospects playing in hundreds of arenas scattered across several countries, it has been an enormous challenge for NHL scouts to accurately rate players hailing from across the

Atlantic. Not to mention, young European players arriving in North America often have to overcome X-factors such as cultural differences, language barriers and the fact they're a long, long way from home.

Narrowing this list down to just 10 late-round gems was tough, too, as evidenced by how many Euro-stars didn't make the cut. Thomas Steen (103rd overall, 1979, Winnipeg), Miikka Kiprusoff (116th, 1995, San Jose), Nikolai Khabibulin (204th, 1992, Winnipeg), Vladimir Konstantinov (221st, 1989, Detroit) and Pavol Demitra (227th, 1993, Ottawa) all come to mind as stellar European NHLers who were claimed in the depths of the draft.

Among the top 10, it's hard to argue with Dominik Hasek at No. 1. Nine rounds went by at the 1983 entry draft before Chicago selected one the greatest goaltenders of all-time. Interestingly, Hasek is one of three 2007-08 Red Wings to make the list; Pavel Datsyuk and Henrik Zetterberg also were passed over by every NHL team for several rounds before ending up in Detroit.

Five-time 50-goal man Pavel Bure and Daniel Alfredsson, who hasn't looked back since winning the Calder Trophy in 1995-96, round out the top three. A couple other notables are Slava Fetisov and Igor Larionov, who spent a decade leading the Central Red Army team in Russia before coming to the NHL in their early 30s.

The **Detroit Red Wings'** Dominik Hasek, Nicklas Lidstrom, Henrik Zetterberg and Pavel Datsyuk

Calgary Flames mascot **Harvey the Hound**

Best Mascots

1. HARVEY THE HOUND
Calgary Flames

2. S.J. SHARKIE
San Jose Sharks

3. WILD WING
Anaheim Ducks

4. YOUPPI!
Montreal Canadiens

5. CARLTON THE BEAR
Toronto Maple Leafs

6. GNASH
Nashville Predators

7. THUNDERBUG
Tampa Bay Lightning

8. THRASH
Atlanta Thrashers

9. STANLEY C. PANTHER
Florida Panthers

10. SPARTACAT
Ottawa Senators

I t's the most famous tongue snatching of all-time.

In an incident that belies the much-celebrated relationship between man and dog, Edmonton Oilers coach Craig MacTavish once ripped the tongue of Flames mascot Harvey the Hound right out of the Calgary canine's furry mouth.

San Jose Sharks mascot **SJ Sharkie**

Seems like an ironic form of retribution given the one thing Harvey never does is verbally hound the visiting team. In his line of work, nobody does.

Still, his antics behind the Oilers bench during a 2003 installment of the Battle of Alberta were enough to incite MacTavish.

But Harvey had his backers. In a show of solidarity for their fellow entertainer, many mascots showed up at the 2003 NHL All-Star Game, held just a few weeks after the incident, with newly attached tongues wagging out.

Montreal fans have been treated to Youppi's antics for many years in all seasons. The ambiguous collection of orange hair worked Montreal Expos baseball games from 1979 until the team moved to Washington in 2004. He was the first mascot to be tossed from a Major League Baseball game (at the behest of Los Angeles Dodgers manager Tommy Lasorda) and is one of three mascots to be honored by baseball's Hall of Fame.

Youppi hasn't missed a beat since moving over to the Bell Centre, thrilling Canadiens fans young and old with his energetic routines.

Best No. 2 Overall ● ● ● Draft Picks

1. CHRIS PRONGER (behind Alexandre Daigle in 1993)
2000 Norris, Hart winner should have won Conn Smythe in '06.

2. MARCEL DIONNE (behind Guy Lafleur in 1971)
Hall of Famer fifth in all-time points, fourth in all-time goals.

3. BRENDAN SHANAHAN (behind Pierre Turgeon in 1987)
600-goal scorer credited for helping to re-inject speed and scoring after NHL lockout with 'Shanahan Summit.'

4. BRIAN BELLOWS (behind Gord Kluzak in 1982)
Nine-time 30-goal man youngest NHLer to ever wear a 'C.'

5. DANY HEATLEY (behind Rick DiPietro in 2000)
First Sen to score 50 also owns all-time goal record at World Championship.

6. KIRK MULLER (behind Mario Lemieux in 1984)
Gritty leader remembered best for Habs' Cup run in 1993.

7. ERIC STAAL (behind Marc-Andre Fleury in 2003)
2006 Cup winner took home MVP honors at '08 All-Star Game.

8. EVGENI MALKIN (behind Alex Ovechkin in 2004)
Russian phenom scored goals in each of his first six NHL games.

9. TREVOR LINDEN (behind Mike Modano in 1988)
Captain Canuck played 14 full seasons – and more than 100 playoff games – for Vancouver.

10. DAVE BABYCH (behind Doug Wickenheiser in 1980)
More than 700 points from the blueline...and a sweet moustache, too.

If the Senators could only turn back the clock. The year was 1993 and all the hype heading into the NHL entry draft surrounded high-scoring Victoriaville (QMJHL) center Alexander Daigle.

Hindsight, as they say, is 20/20.

The top selection looks more absurd with each passing season as that year's second overall pick – Chris Pronger – continues to build his case for the Hall of Fame while Daigle's NHL days are long gone and better forgotten.

Known as much for his nasty streak as his offensive and defensive prowess, Pronger has a Hart and Norris Trophy to his name and helped the Ducks to a Stanley Cup championship in 2007, one year after leading the underdog Oilers to within one game of hockey's ultimate glory.

Chris Pronger

Early on, however, it looked as though Pronger's career would fare no better than Daigle's.

A lax approach to training and a few minor run-ins with the law magnified Pronger's struggles on the ice as the Hartford Whalers missed the playoffs in both of Pronger's first two campaigns.

It wasn't until he arrived in St. Louis – and a date with hard-line coach Mike Keenan – for the 1995-96 season that the 6-foot-6, 220-pound behemoth realized a little elbow grease often triumphs a lot of skill.

"I had just come from Hartford, which was a nightmare, and here I was in St. Louis...I'm 21 years old and Mike Keenan is beating me into the ground," Pronger told The Hockey News in 2007. "I was lost.

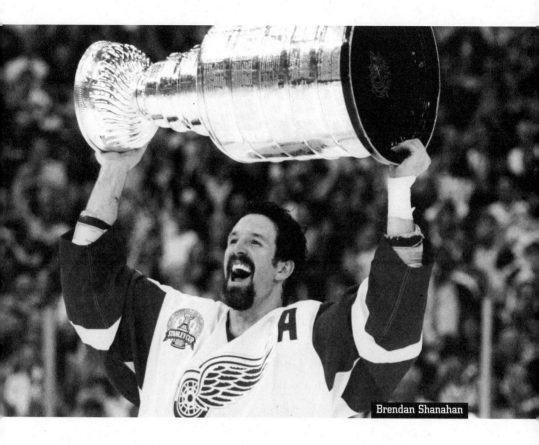

Brendan Shanahan

"When you're as competitive as I am and you don't like losing, well, I just felt like I was losing. That's when I started really working hard off the ice and I turned things around."

And how. Besides his decorated NHL career, Pronger has also starred for Team Canada on the international stage, suiting up at three Olympics, winning gold in 2002 at Salt Lake City.

Suspensions and trade requests aside, Pronger's legacy will be that of one of the game's great blueliners and shortly after he hangs them up he'll join Marcel Dionne (and, likely, Brendan Shanahan) as No. 2 overall draft picks in the Hall of Fame.

Best Late-Round ● ● ●
North American
Draft Picks

1. BRETT HULL
117th overall, 1984, Calgary

2. LUC ROBITAILLE
171st overall, 1984, Los Angeles

3. DOUG GILMOUR
134th overall, 1982, St. Louis

4. STEVE LARMER
120th overall, 1980, Chicago

5. RON HEXTALL
119th overall, 1982, Philadelphia

6. THEOREN FLEURY
166th overall, 1987, Calgary

7. RICK TOCCHET
125th overall, 1983, Philadelphia

8. GARY SUTER
180th overall, 1984, Calgary

9. DAVE TAYLOR
210th overall, 1975, Los Angeles

10. ANDY MOOG
132nd overall, 1980, Edmonton

Steve Larmer

Don't try telling these players that drafting is an exact science. This list of NHLers who were nearly forgotten as prospects contains some of the league's all-time leading goal-scorers, such as 1984 draftees Brett Hull and Luc Robitaille.

While most players selected after the first round – and heck, most players picked in the first round, too – don't go on to have long, prolific NHL careers, there are always a few who leave scouts scratching their heads with a surprising rise to prominence.

Take Steve Larmer, for example. A high-scoring right winger for his hometown Peterborough Petes and Niagara Falls Flyers, Larmer racked up 247 points in 128 games over his final two seasons in the OHL. However, he wasn't projected to relay those skills to the NHL. But he did – and it didn't take long. Larmer amassed 42 goals and 90 points for Chicago in 1981-82 en route to winning the Calder Trophy as the NHL's best rookie. And he didn't miss a single contest during his first 11 NHL campaigns – that's 884 consecutive games, folks – a stretch in which he scored at least 30 goals nine times (and at least 40 goals five times). Not bad for a sixth-round pick who was taken 117 spots behind his longtime Hawks linemate, Denis Savard.

Worst ● ● ● ● ● ●
NHL Teams Of All-Time

1. 1974-75 WASHINGTON CAPITALS
8-67-5 record, .131 win pct.

2. 1992-93 OTTAWA SENATORS
10-70-4 record, .143 win pct.

3. 1992-93 SAN JOSE SHARKS
11-71-2 record, .143 win pct.

4. 1972-73 NY ISLANDERS
12-60-6 record, .192 win pct.

5. 1943-44 NY RANGERS
6-39-5 record, .170 win pct.

6. 1989-90 QUEBEC NORDIQUES
12-61-7 record, .194 win pct.

7. 1928-29 CHICAGO BLACK HAWKS
7-29-8 record, .250 win pct.

8. 1980-81 WINNIPEG JETS
9-57-14 record, .200 win pct.

9. 1975-76 KANSAS CITY SCOUTS
12-56-12 record, .225 win pct.

10. 1953-54 CHICAGO BLACK HAWKS
12-51-7 record, .221 win pct.

How bad were these 10 teams? The 1980-81 Winnipeg Jets had a 30-game winless streak – and they barely made the list, at No. 8. The 1928-29 Chicago Black Hawks take the No. 7 spot for the ignominious distinction of being the only team in history to score less than a goal per game (33 in 44 games). And the 1943-44 New York Rangers had a higher goals-against average (6.2) than they had wins (six) in a 50-game schedule. For this, they crack the top five.

But the dubious "worst team of all-time" title belongs to the truly terrible 1974-75 Washington Capitals. In their infamous inaugural season, the Caps set records for futility with 17 straight losses (which still stands) and 37 consecutive road losses, a mark that lasted close to 20 years until the No. 2 team on the list, the 1992-93 Ottawa Senators, lost the first 38 road games of their first NHL campaign.

Not only did Washington have the lowest winning percentage in league history at .131, the Capitals set the wrong kinds of records for most goals against in a season (446) and all-time worst goal differential (minus-265). They allowed 5.6 goals per game – about 3.3 more than they scored – and all those goals came against two beleaguered netminders, Ron Low and Michel Belhumeur. Poor Belhumeur went 0-24-3 in '74-75 and 0-5-1 the next season, which mercifully was his last in the NHL.

Mike
Bloom

Brett Hull's Cup-winning goal in 1999 was big news in **Dallas**... but **not** in **Buffalo**.

• • • Greatest
Overtime Moments

1. BOSTON BRUINS 4, ST. LOUIS BLUES 3
May 10, 1970 (0:40 of the first overtime period)

Bobby Orr scores the Stanley Cup-clinching goal in Game 4 and then gets airborne, creating one of the most iconic photographs in sport. The goal gives the Bruins their first championship in 29 years and cements Orr's legacy as one of the most beloved sports figures in Boston history.

2. TORONTO MAPLE LEAFS 3, MONTREAL CANADIENS 2
April 21, 1951 (2:53 of the first overtime period)

Bill Barilko scores in Game 5 — the fifth game in a row that went to extra time — to win the Cup for the Leafs. Barilko disappears that summer when his plane goes down while returning from a fishing trip in northern Quebec.

3. DETROIT RED WINGS 4, NEW YORK RANGERS 3
April 23, 1950 (8:31 of the second overtime period)

Pete Babando scores the winner in the first Stanley Cup final Game 7 to go to overtime. Four years later, another Red Wing — Tony Leswick — pots the game-winner in the last Cup final to go to overtime in Game 7.

4. NEW YORK ISLANDERS 5, PHILADELPHIA FLYERS 4
May 24, 1980 (7:11 of the first overtime period)

Bob Nystrom swats in the series winner in Game 6 of the final for the Islanders, starting a run of four consecutive Cups for the first dynasty of the 1980s.

5. DALLAS STARS 2, BUFFALO SABRES 1
June 19, 1999 (14:51 of the third overtime period)

With a skate in the crease, Brett Hull scores the infamous 'No Goal' goal in Game 6, breaking the hearts of Buffalo fans and delivering Dallas its first and only Stanley Cup. The controversial "skate in the crease" rule is relaxed the next season, but Sabres fans are still reeling from what was clearly — according to the rules at the time — an illegal goal.

6. NEW YORK ISLANDERS 4, PITTSBURGH PENGUINS 3
May 14, 1993 (5:16 of the first overtime period)

Pittsburgh finishes first overall and are the odds-on favorite to capture their third straight Cup. But with Glenn Healy stoning the Pens during this second round Game 7 classic and the oft-scratched David Volek providing two goals (including the overtime winner), the Islanders pull off a stunning upset.

7. MONTREAL CANADIENS 3, CALGARY FLAMES 2
May 18, 1986 (0:09 of the first overtime period)

Brian Skrudland wastes little time recording the fastest overtime goal in NHL playoff history during Game 2 of the final; the Canadiens go on to capture their 23rd Stanley Cup in five games. Calgary gets redemption three years later, beating Montreal for the Flames' only Cup in 1989.

8. PITTSBURGH PENGUINS 4, DETROIT RED WINGS 3
June 2, 2008 (9:57 of the third overtime period)

After squandering a 2-0 first period lead in Game 5 of the Cup final, the Pens score with 35 seconds left in the third period to force overtime. Two-and-a-half scoreless periods later, Petr Sykora scores from the right faceoff circle to keep the series alive – after telling his teammates he'd notch the game-winner between the first and second overtimes.

9. NEW YORK ISLANDERS 3, WASHINGTON CAPITALS 2
April 18, 1987 (8:47 of the fourth overtime period)

During the first round, Pat LaFontaine's seeing-eye slapper from the top of the faceoff circle ends the longest Game 7 in NHL history. Islanders goalie Kelly Hrudey makes an incredible 73 saves in backstopping his team to the victory, while Caps netminder Bob Mason stops a mere 54 shots.

10. PITTSBURGH PENGUINS 3, WASHINGTON CAPITALS 2
April 24, 1996 (19:15 of the fourth overtime period)

Petr Nedved ends the fifth-longest contest in NHL history in Game 4 of the first round, spurring the Penguins on to a conference final appearance. Four years later, Pens players feel the sting of losing a marathon game when Keith Primeau scores for the Philadelphia Flyers to end the third-longest game in history at 12:01 of the fifth overtime.

Best ● ● ● ● ● ●
Undrafted NHLers

1. WAYNE GRETZKY
2,857 career NHL points

2. PETER STASTNY
Second-most points in 1980s behind Gretzky

3. BORJE SALMING
Pioneering European NHLer

4. ED BELFOUR
Third-most wins all-time with 484

5. ADAM OATES
Sixth-most assists all-time with 1,079

6. DINO CICCARELLI
608 goals

7. MARTIN ST-LOUIS
Won Art Ross, Hart and Stanley Cup in 2004

8. TIM KERR
Four consecutive 50-plus goal seasons in mid-1980s

9. CURTIS JOSEPH
Fourth-most wins all-time with 449

10. STEVE THOMAS
421 goals, 933 points in 20-year career

The NHL entry draft isn't exactly a perfect process. Occasionally, a good player slips through the cracks and isn't selected at all. Brian Rafalski, Dan Boyle, Niklas Backstrom, Andy McDonald and Sean Avery are just a few examples of active NHLers who were never drafted.

No one believed Martin St-Louis could hold up in the NHL with his diminutive frame, but the University of Vermont grad parlayed an excellent NCAA career into a free agency deal with Calgary and eventually a Hart Trophy and Stanley Cup with Tampa Bay. Other college boys who had to fight perception problems include all-time great playmaker Adam Oates (despite 150 assists and 216 points in 98 games with R.P.I.) and goalies Ed Belfour and Curtis Joseph, who suited up for North Dakota and Wisconsin, respectively.

Other players were in the major junior spotlight, but didn't catch the eyes necessary when they were 18. Dino Ciccarelli, Steve Thomas and Tim Kerr each joined NHL teams as free agents – and each scored goals at a remarkable frequency once they made it to the big leagues.

Before Europeans were accepted into the fabric of the North American game, several teams got absolute steals by sticking their necks out on a guy from the other side of the Atlantic. Borje Salming provided the Toronto Maple Leafs with more

Wayne Gretzky

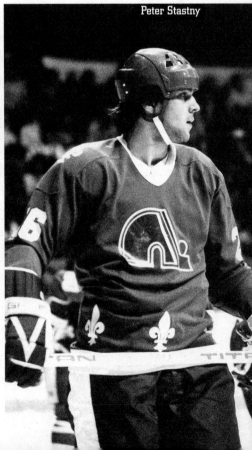
Peter Stastny

than a decade of superlative service, while Peter Stastny proved to be the best player ever during the Quebec Nordiques era of that organization. These two dynamic Hall of Famers faced a lot of prejudice and adversity from NHLers who didn't like the idea of Europeans in "their" league, but Salming and Stastny overcame all obstacles en route to superstardom.

And of course, there's Wayne Gretzky. It's not that nobody wanted The Great One; he simply was already under contract and playing pro hockey. Back in the carefree days of the World Hockey Association, Indianapolis Racers owner Nelson Skalbania signed the 17-year-old Brantford, Ont., wunderkind to a special "personal services" deal in 1978 to beat the rest of the hockey world to the punch. Ironically, even having Gretzky on the squad wasn't enough to keep the Racers viable in Indianapolis and the teen phenom was sold to another WHA franchise, the Edmonton Oilers. When the Oilers joined the NHL soon after, Gretzky began to tear up a whole new league – even though he hadn't been drafted into the circuit.

Borje Salming

Martin St-Louis

High-Profile ● ● ●
Wives

1. JANET JONES
Hollywood star's vow exchange with Wayne Gretzky treated
like a royal wedding in Canada.

2. ANNA KOURNIKOVA
Tennis sexpot married for short period to Russian great Sergei Fedorov.

3. CAROL ALT
Supermodel once married to former NHLer Ron Greschner,
now with ex-Islander Alexei Yashin.

4. KRISTI YAMAGUCHI
Olympic gold medalist in figure skating partnered up with
veteran NHL blueliner Bret Hedican.

5. ANGELICA BRIDGES
Baywatch actress, model fell for Oilers D-man Sheldon Souray.

6. KIM ALEXIS
Elite model married former Rangers star Ron Duguay.

7. TERRI WELLES
Playboy's 1981 Playmate of The Year and former Kings winger
Charlie Simmer had five-year marriage.

8. CANDACE CAMERON
Full House actress has been hitched to ex-Panther Valeri Bure since 1996.

9. MADOLYN SMITH
Former TV/movie actress also the wife of former
Maple Leaf/Ranger Mark Osborne.

10. GENA LEE NOLIN
Price Is Right and Baywatch beauty said "I do" with journeyman
Cale Hulse in 2004.

Bret Hedican and Kristi Yamaguchi

Anna Kournikova and Sergei Fedorov

Hockey players have long enjoyed the attentions of beautiful women. Some of those women, though, have been the recipients of much attention themselves.

For starters, there's Janet Jones, an actress (*The Flamingo Kid, A Chorus Line*) who dated tennis star Vitas Gerulaitis and actor Bruce Willis before falling in love with Oilers center Wayne Gretzky in the mid-'80s.

Everyone knew Jones' name after she married Gretzky, but most people already knew Anna Kournikova's name by the time The Hockey News broke the story that she and Detroit Red Wings great Sergei Fedorov were married briefly.

Another woman who made a name for herself before marrying into the hockey world was Carol Alt, a globetrotting model who exchanged vows with former Ranger Ron Greschner in 1983. The couple divorced 13 years later, and Alt soon started a relationship with former Islanders captain Alexei Yashin.

Kristi Yamaguchi is the only athlete who appears on this list. But what an athlete: 1992 Olympic gold medal-winning figure skater, two-time world champion – and a winner on the hit TV show *Dancing With The Stars*.

Two *Baywatch* alumni members, Angelica Bridges and Gena Lee Nolin, are on the list, and they share another career achievement – posing nude for *Playboy Magazine* – with Terri Welles, Charlie Simmer's ex-wife.

Honorable mentions go to Mike Modano's wife Willa Ford (who played Anna Nicole Smith in a recent biopic); elite model Veronika Varekova, who married Petr Nedved in 2004; Amy Gilmour, Doug's wife (she had a small role in Canadian TV drama *Degrassi High*); Jennifer Russell, wife of Wade Belak (from the TV hit *Saved By The Bell*); and, Stacia Robitaille, recording artist and wife of retired Kings winger Luc Robitaille.

Celebrity ● ● ● ●
Hockey Fans

1. DENIS LEARY
Actor/comedian/Bruins fan hosts an annual celebrity hockey game in Boston.

2. MIKE MYERS
Austin Powers star made his beloved Maple Leafs a central focus in Love Guru movie.

3. JERRY BRUCKHEIMER
Wildly successful TV/movie producer rumored to be interested in bringing an NHL franchise to Las Vegas.

4. KID ROCK
Michigan-area rocker close friends with many Red Wings veterans.

5. PAT SAJAK
Wheel Of Fortune host was swept up by Capitals mania in 2008 playoffs.

6. VINCE GILL AND AMY GRANT
High-profile Predators fans are one of country music's top husband-and-wife teams.

7. LIL JON
Atlanta-based rap star also a big-time Thrashers booster.

8. KURT RUSSELL AND GOLDIE HAWN
Russell played Herb Brooks in Miracle movie; their son Wyatt tended goal for a Canadian Jr. A team.

9. KEVIN SMITH
Movie director loves his New Jersey Devils.

10. CHRISTIE BRINKLEY
Supermodel, New York Islanders fan blogged about team during '07-08 season.

Celebrity hockey fans are very much like the rest of us — except they usually don't wince when confronted with the NHL's exorbitant ticket prices (in reality, they probably get their seats for free). They still have their favorite teams, players and hockey memories, though, and still have their inner child come out when they get the opportunity to meet their favorite stars. From Tim Robbins to Alex Trebek, Snoop Dogg to Garth Brooks and Steve Carell to Carol Alt, famous faces can be found off the ice at NHL rinks, too.

Lil John

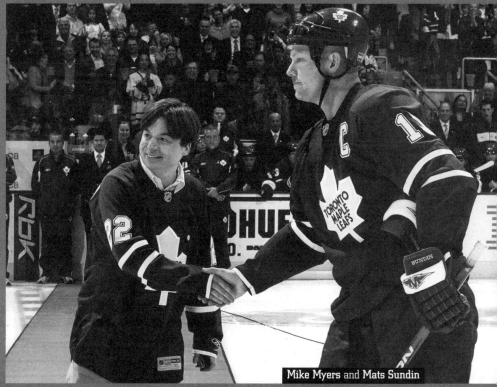

Mike Myers and Mats Sundin

Unbreakable ● ● ●
Records

1. GLENN HALL'S 502 CONSECUTIVE GAMES PLAYED
2. WAYNE GRETZKY'S COLLECTIVE RECORDS
3. NEW YORK ISLANDERS' 19 CONSECUTIVE PLAYOFF SERIES VICTORIES FROM 1980-84
4. MONTREAL CANADIENS' EIGHT LOSSES IN 1976-77
5. TEEMU SELANNE'S 76 GOALS AS A ROOKIE IN 1992-93
6. BILL MOSIENKO'S 21-SECOND HAT TRICK ON MARCH 23, 1952
7. BOBBY ORR'S 139 POINTS BY A DEFENSEMAN AND PLUS-124 RATING IN 1970-71
8. DARRYL SITTLER'S 10-POINT GAME ON FEB. 7, 1976
9. EDMONTON OILERS' 446 GOALS SCORED IN 1983-84
10. PATRICK ROY'S 151 PLAYOFF VICTORIES

Truth be told, we could have filled this list entirely with Wayne Gretzky's records. For the man who holds or shares 61 NHL records (which in itself is a record), nothing is impossible. His career was a giant hyperbole. Most career goals (894), assists (1,963) and points (2,857) are just the tip of the iceberg. How about 13 consecutive 100-plus point seasons? Can the young and talented Sidney Crosby or Alex Ovechkin match that high-caliber consistency? What about Gretzky's 92-goal campaign in 1981-82? Or the 163 assists and 215 points he put up in 1985-86? Not to mention, 47 points in just 18 playoff games in 1984-85. It says a lot about these records when you consider that 50 goals in 39 games seems downright attainable by comparison. Gretzky had five consecutive seasons of 60-plus goals, 12 straight years of 40-plus goals and four seasons in which he scored over 200 points. Nobody else has hit 200 points even once, though Mario Lemieux came oh-so-close in 1988-89 with 199. Gretzky also had 50 hat tricks in his career, including nine four-goal games and four five-goal games. And to top it all off, he owns the longest point streak, too: a 51-gamer in 1983-84 in which he racked up 61 goals and 153 points.

Wayne Gretzky

Best Hockey Books

1. THE HOCKEY SWEATER
Roch Carrier's heartwarming tale strikes a chord with all readers, even those who aren't Habs fans.

2. NET WORTH: EXPLODING THE MYTHS OF PRO HOCKEY
David Cruise and Alison Griffiths explore the exploitation of former NHLers and how the players rose to stop it.

3. THE GAME
Ken Dryden's memoirs considered the best hockey book ever written.

4. TOTAL HOCKEY
A treasure trove of information for the hockey geek in all of us.

5. LIONS IN WINTER
Chrys Goyens and Allan Turowetz pen the ultimate intellectual biography of the Montreal Canadiens.

6. GROSS MISCONDUCT
Martin O'Malley chronicles the troubled life and death of former NHLer Brian 'Spinner' Spencer.

7. THE HOCKEY HANDBOOK
Lloyd Percival's 1951 scientific study of the sport was a favorite of Anatoli Tarasov, the father of Soviet hockey.

8. WHEN THE LIGHTS WENT OUT
Gare Joyce's chronicle of the Piestany Punch-Up at the 1987 World Junior Championship is painstakingly researched and well-written.

9. THE SCOTT YOUNG TRILOGY
Scrubs on Skates, Boy on Defence and *A Boy at Leafs' Camp* are must-reads for any young hockey fan.

10. SAVED: A NOVEL
Jack Falla gives us hockey's first great work of fiction.

The ultimate irony is the tiny town of Ste-Justine, Que., has produced only one NHL player – Alex Tanguay of the Montreal Canadiens.

But Ste-Justine is also the setting for the most classic piece of literature in hockey history, *The Hockey Sweater* by Roch Carrier. Ste-Justine is Carrier's hometown and *The Hockey Sweater* represents a real-life account of his childhood experience from the winter of 1946.

Carrier and his friends are obsessed with Canadiens star Maurice Richard, who by this time has become a cultural touchstone for Francophone Quebeckers. When they played hockey outdoors, "We were five Maurice Richards against five other Maurice Richards…We were 10 players all wearing the uniform of the Montreal Canadiens, all with the same burning enthusiasm."

Young Roch's Richard sweater wears out and when his mother orders a replacement from Eaton's, a department store that represents the bastion of English Canada, he instead receives a Toronto Maple Leafs sweater.

Humiliated, he is forced to play wearing the Maple Leafs sweater and when he receives a game misconduct in his next outing, the referee/priest tells him to go to church to pray for forgiveness.

The young boy goes to church and prays to God to "send to me right away 100 million moths that would eat my Toronto Maple Leafs sweater."

The book was originally published in French as *Le chandail de hockey* and was released in English in 1979. A year later, the National Film Board in Canada made it an animated film entitled *The Sweater*.

Logos We Miss ● ● ●

1. MINNESOTA NORTH STARS (1967-93)

The beauty is in the simplicity.
An 'N' and a star, in green and gold.

2. ATLANTA FLAMES (1972-80)

Sure, Calgary followed the template, but nothing beats
the original flame-inside-the-letter design.

3. LOS ANGELES KINGS (1967-75)

Why is everyone so afraid to use color today?
The purple-and-gold crown made an impact.

4. KANSAS CITY SCOUTS (1974-76)

A guy, a horse and hockey. The unnatural hat trick.

5. HARTFORD WHALERS (1979-97)

Distinct and straightforward. See No. 3
about color use.

6. QUEBEC NORDIQUES (1979-95)

The Picasso of old logos. A stick, a puck and that other thing...a
mouse house? An igloo? Dan Bouchard's five-hole?

7. COLORADO ROCKIES (1976-82)

Hmm...wonder if the second-grader who
designed it is still collecting royalties?

8. CALIFORNIA GOLDEN SEALS (1974-76)

The logo says it all. Literally. Plus, it reminds
us of white skates.

9. CLEVELAND BARONS (1976-78)

Anything that institutes a classic,
old English font is OK by us.

10. NEW YORK ISLANDERS (1996-97)

Fishermen are scary. Make that scary funny.

PAST.
PRESENT.
FUTURE.

The Hockey News commemorates 60 years of tradition with two fabulous new collectible books.

The Top 60 Since 1967 identifies the top 60 players of the NHL since the league expanded 40 years ago. The list was voted on and selected by a panel of experts that includes former and current NHL executives, members of the media and the editors at The Hockey News.

Hockey's Young Guns details the rise of 25 of hockey's most prominent young stars and what it took them to make it to the NHL.

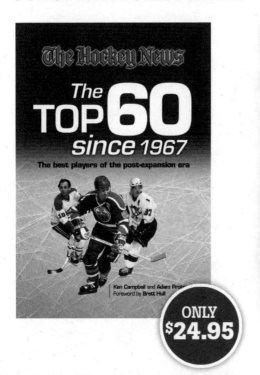

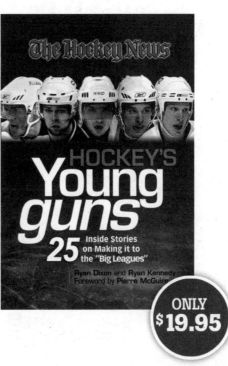

Available at a bookstore near you or visit thehockeynews.com

The Hockey News